The Fearless International Foodie

Conquers Pan-Asian Cuisine

- Japanese
- Lao
- Cambodian
- Malaysian
- Indonesian
- Thai
- Vietnamese
- Korean

David d'Aprix

LIVING LANGUAGE®

A DIVISION OF RANDOM HOUSE

Acknowledgments

Many thanks to the Living Language staff: Lisa Alpert, Elizabeth Bennett, Chris Warnasch, Zviezdana Verzich, Suzanne McQuade, Helen Tang, Mary Lee, Fernando Galeano, Sophie Chin, Denise De-Gennaro, Marina Padakis, Holly McKinley, and Pat Ehresmann. Special thanks to Fuhito Shimoyama, Manorom Phonseya, Saleumxay Kommasith, Ung Sovannary, May Wanhamid, Puchong Boontycoon, Nga Nguyen, and Seungwan Yoon.

Published by Living Language, a division of Random House, Inc., New York

Random House, Inc. New York, Toronto, London, Sydney, Auckland

Living Language is a registered trademark of Random House, Inc.

Manufactured in the United States of America

Interior design by Sophie Ye Chin

ISBN 0-609-80657-2

10   9   8   7   6   5   4   3   2   1

First Edition

The Fearless

International

Foodie

ALSO BY DAVID D'APRIX

The Fearless International Foodie Conquers
the Cuisine of France,
Italy, Spain & Latin America

International Foreign Language
Guide for Hotel Employees

TABLE OF CONTENTS

Japanese Cuisine

Pan-Asian Cuisine: Laos, Cambodia, Malaysia, and Indonesia

CONTENTS

Thai Cuisine

Vietnamese Cuisine

Korean Cuisine

Introduction

The Fearless International Foodie Conquers Pan-Asian Cuisine will help you enjoy Asian food without embarrassment and frustration. You'll acquire a wonderful sense of each cuisine in a concise format, with no special knowledge needed of the languages involved. If you don't know your *pajon* from your *basmati,* your *kimchi* from your *kecap,* or your *sushi* from your *satay,* this is the book for you. The popularity of Asian foods is growing every day, so give yourself a head start now with this portable guide.

    The Fearless International Foodie Conquers Pan-Asian Cuisine is divided by cuisine into five sections: Japanese, Pan-Asian (Lao, Cambodian, Malaysian, and Indonesian), Thai, Vietnamese, and Korean. Each section begins with an overview of the cuisine and its peculiarities, then lists several representative dishes. A glossary at the end of each section allows you to look up individual ingredients and preparations. All of the languages in this guide use writing systems different from our own, so the words you see here act as a pronunciation guide in themselves. If you get stuck, use the appendix in the back of the book to aid your pronunciation so you can order a dish in a way that a native speaker will understand.

    Although this guide is extremely useful when taken into a restaurant or for deciphering a menu in the comfort of your home, we hope that's not the only way you'll use it. Just flip to a cuisine, read about its characteristics, and enjoy browsing through the variety of dishes. You'll soon find yourself understanding the seasonings and cooking techniques used. Those are the two key aspects to understanding any cuisine, and having a sense of the cooking philosophy aids a great deal in enjoying new foods.

The notes and tips throughout the book will guide you in absorbing some of the customs of the particular country, and you'll feel more at home in an Asian restaurant. It's fascinating to see how little things such as eating utensils can change as you move throughout Asia. Using proper table manners and ordering like a native will enhance your dining experience. However, please don't be intimidated, even if you don't feel entirely comfortable with the menu and customs. Any restaurant is eager to show you their food, and if you just ask your server for recommendations, you can enjoy the foods as if it were old hat.

You'll be a fearless foodie in no time!

Japanese Cuisine

WELCOME TO THE DELIGHTFUL SIMPLICITY of Japanese food. The delicious tastes of Japan derive from an insistence on only the freshest, highest-quality ingredients. Wonderful flavors result from a minimum of seasoning and cooking. Plate presentations and artistic garnishes provide the visual stimulation to accompany the great flavors. Voilà! Or should we say, *Sa!*

Indeed, Japanese cuisine, or *ryori,* is the very embodiment of subtlety and simplicity, although preparations are far from easy. Japanese chefs are highly trained and skilled. With sublime ability they strive toward exacting the essence from ingredients rather than adding layers of flavors that cover up their natural purity.

In Japan, some restaurants serve *Nihon-ryori* (general Japanese cuisine), which is essentially what Japanese restaurants in America serve.

Overview of Japanese Dining

THERE ARE MANY STYLES OF DINING and many levels of formality. In Japan most restaurants specialize in one type of food. In the United States, however, most Japanese restaurants will offer several styles of food under the same roof. Nonetheless, the categories provide a convenient way to understand the structure of Japanese cuisine. Each category is a subspecialty with its own particular rules and flavors.

Typical restaurant/cuisine types include *teppanyaki* (grilled steaks and other foods cooked tableside), *sushi* (raw fish with rice and other ingredients), *unagi* (eel), *fugu* (blowfish), *tempura* (batter-fried foods), *soba* and *udon* (buckwheat and wheat noodles), *tonkatsu* (deep-fried pork cutlets), *kushiage* (skewered foods), *yakitori* (grilled chicken), *kamameshi* (rice dishes), *nabemono* (quick-cooked stews), *sukiyaki* and *shabu-shabu* (beef hot pot dishes), *oden* (fish-dumpling stews), *miso* (soy and grain paste), and *okonomiyaki* (Japanese savory pancakes).

NOTE Using chopsticks is the normal way to eat most Japanese food. Chopsticks are a pleasant break from a fork and knife, but be sure to practice your technique. When using the *waribashi*, or disposable wood chopsticks offered in most restaurants, you should remove them from the bag or paper envelope under the table away from others' eyes. Then pull them apart, still out of sight. Finally, rub them together to smooth away the splinters.

WHAT'S THAT TOWEL?

You will probably be served a hot towel before your meal begins. Use it to wash your hands. Many people use the towel to wash their face, but this is considered rude. You may use it throughout the meal as a napkin. In Japan, napkins are seldom used, though they're invariably supplied in America.

Teppanyaki

(Grilled steaks and other foods cooked tableside)

MANY AMERICANS FIRST EXPERIENCE Japanese food at these delightful, entertaining restaurants, where you sit with other people in a big booth, with a flat grill by the table. The chef slices the meat and vegetables at the table, handling the knife with amazing agility. The food is then grilled in front of the guests, seasoned lightly, and served. Simple cooking with the freshest ingredients—that's Japanese.

Teppanyaki is a modern Japanese concept, and it is greatly overshadowed in America today by the popularity of *sushi* bars. However, we include this style of food first because of the big splash it made several years ago, and also because it's simple, fun, and delicious.

NOTE When eating your rice, don't hold the bowl close to your mouth and shovel in the rice. This is considered rude. Chopsticks are hard to use, but practice makes perfect.

Hire suteki	Fillet
Hotategai	Scallops
Ika	Squid

Kinoko	Mushrooms
Kuruma-ebi	Prawns
Maromi suteki	Steak with *miso*
Mikkusu guriru	Mixed grill
Nama-shiitake	Fresh *shiitake* mushrooms
Piman	Green pepper
Sarada	Salad
Saroin suteki	Sirloin steak
Teppanyaki	Grilled

Sushi

SUSHI HAS BECOME INCREDIBLY POPULAR around the world. It is undoubtedly Japan's most famous food. Again, flavors are subtle, so the absolutely freshest and highest-quality ingredients are essential. Most commonly, *sushi* is raw fish with vinegared rice, *wasabi* (Japanese horseradish), and soy sauce. The one constant in all *sushi* is the rice seasoned with sweetened rice vinegar. Raw fish is normal but not necessary, as some *sushi* has no fish at all or uses cooked seafood. The visual delight in the beautiful presentation of fish on mounds of rice adds immensely to the simple flavors. *Sushi* is an experience that transcends simple eating.

Long, intense training is required to become a sushi *chef. Shaping the rice is in itself incredibly difficult, and slicing the fish paper-thin is no job for a beginner! The best place to eat* sushi, *either in the United States or in Japan, is at a* sushi *bar, where it's freshest and prepared by the most skilled chefs.*

NOTE Proper etiquette demands that *sushi* be eaten in one bite!

Sashimi is served at a sushi *bar, but* sashimi *is simply raw fish, often served as an appetizer. Beautiful arrangements of* sashimi, *often made to look like flowers, entice the palate.*

Types of Sushi

MAKI-ZUSHI OR NORI-MAKI

YOU MAY KNOW THESE as "California rolls." This is the *sushi* that is wrapped in a sheet of *nori*, which is a type of seaweed. Many people think this is *sushi*, because it's prevalent even in supermarkets. There is a lot of vinegared rice surrounding a few ingredients, not even necessarily fish. The ingredients, whether crabmeat, avocado, or cucumber, are rolled inside a sheet of *nori*. Sometimes, the *nori* is wrapped around the ingredients, and the rice surrounds that. *Nori-maki* is made by placing a sheet of toasted *nori* on a bamboo roller, putting vinegared rice on top, and then adding the ingredients that go inside, including vegetables and seafood. The whole thing is rolled up, then sliced into conveniently sized rounds.

Kaiware-maki	*Daikon*-sprout roll
Kappa-maki	Cucumber-filled roll
Negitoro-maki	Scallion and tuna roll
Shinko-maki	Pickled *daikon* (Japanese radish)-filled roll
Tekka-maki	Tuna-filled roll
Temaki	Similar to *maki-zushi*, but rolled by hand into cone shapes
Umejiso-maki	*Ume* plum and perilla leaf roll

NIGIRI-ZUSHI

Other than the *maki-zushi*, *nigiri-zushi* is probably the best known—it's elegantly presented, seafood-covered, molded rice. First, the rice is molded by hand (a very highly skilled job), then it is seasoned with a bit of *wasabi* and covered with the seafood. It is eaten with the fingers or with chopsticks, and is dipped very briefly in soy sauce. *Nigiri-zushi* comes from Tokyo and is also called *Edomae-zushi* (Edo was the name for Tokyo before 1868).

Ama-ebi	Raw shrimp
Anago	Conger eel
Awabi	Abalone
Ebi	Cooked shrimp
Gari	Sliced, pickled ginger used as a condiment for *sushi*
Hamagur	Clam
Hirame	Flounder
Hotategai	Scallops
Ika	Squid
Ikura	Salmon roe
Inada	Very young yellowtail
Kaiware	*Daikon* sprouts
Katsuo	Bonito
Kazunoko	Herring roe
Kuruma-ebi	Prawns
Maguro	Tuna
Ni-ika	Squid cooked in a broth
Otoro	Fat portion of tuna
Saba	Mackerel
Suzuki	Sea bass
Tako	Octopus
Tamago	Sweet egg custard in seaweed
Torigai	Cockle
Toro	Best part of the tuna belly
Uni	Sea urchin roe

CHIRASHI-ZUSHI

Chirashi-zushi is a simple type of *sushi* made in all Japanese kitchens. *Chirashi-zushi* is simply *sashimi* and mixed ingredients (egg, pickles, mushrooms, vegetables) in or on vinegared rice. *Chirashi-zushi* can also be made without *sashimi,* and is especially popular at railway station lunch counters, as a convenient lunch away from home.

OSHI-ZUSHI

Oshi-zushi is a speciality of Osaka. It is made by putting the *sushi* rice in a large mold and pressing the fish on top. When it is unmolded, it is cut into bite-sized pieces.

INARI-ZUSHI

Inari-zushi is rice and vegetables wrapped in a pouch of fried *tofu*.

Unagi (Eel)

WHILE YOU WON'T FIND many Japanese restaurants in the United States devoted exclusively to eel, you can easily enjoy eel at many Japanese restaurants. The best places keep live eels on hand and don't begin to prepare the eel until you've ordered, so it takes a bit longer. Typically, the eel is grilled, then steamed to remove the fat, then grilled again, using a sweet basting sauce to create a crispy skin and a soft, tender interior.

Some of us more sheltered Americans have trouble getting past the thought of eating an eel. But if you thought you were eating a less "exotic" kind of fish, you'd probably enjoy this style of preparation immensely. It's sort of like when you were told you were eating chicken, but it was really frog legs. So if you're someone who gets the creeps thinking about those squirmy little devils, try to imagine something like fillet of sole, and take a taste from someone else's plate. Really, you'll be glad you did.

Dojo	Loach, a small type of eel
Kabayaki	Grilled eel on skewers
Kimoyaki	Grilled eel livers served with grated radish
Shirayaki	Eel grilled without sauce
Unagi teishoku **or** *unagi* *zukushi*	Complete meal consisting of grilled eel, eel liver soup, rice, and pickles
Uzaku	Grilled eel and cucumber in a soy vinegar sauce
Yanagawa-nabe	A casserole made with *dojo*, burdock root, and egg
Yawata-maki	Grilled eel rolled around burdock strips

Fugu (Blowfish)

ONLY TRAINED CHEFS IN SPECIALLY licensed restaurants in Japan serve *fugu*, the legendary Japanese blowfish. That's because a toxin in its internal organs can kill you if the fish is improperly prepared. Otherwise, the fish is fine, if not really worth all the brouhaha and expense of serving and eating it. More of the appeal seems to be from the danger than from the taste.

Fugu restaurants start the meal off with *fugu sashimi*, then usually move on to a one-pot meal similar to *shabu-shabu*, then finish with a soup dish. *Fugu* restaurants are quite uncommon in the United States.

Fugu chiri	Blowfish and vegetables, basically *shabu-shabu*
Fugu sashi	Raw blowfish (*sashimi*)
Fugu zosui	Rice porridge with *fugu* broth
Hirezake	Blowfish fins, toasted, served in *sake*

Tempura (Batter-fried foods)

AH, TEMPURA. To many people, *tempura* represents the absolute epitome of Japanese cooking: delicious food that embodies subtlety, beauty, and freshness. What other fried food is so light and airy without a bit of greasiness? Of course, not every restaurant can produce those results, but *tempura* at its best is just that. The best way to eat *tempura* is to sit in front of the chef and eat it as soon as it's cool enough not to burn your mouth.

Tempura was introduced to Japan by the Portuguese in

the 16th century, and the Japanese refined the process until, finally, in the 20th century, *tempura* reached perfection.

The best way to eat *tempura* is to dip it very briefly into the dipping sauce. The sauce is made from *dashi* (stock made from fish and kelp), *mirin* (sweetened *sake* used for cooking), soy sauce, and grated *daikon*. Some aficionados prefer to eat *tempura* with just a little lemon and salt. The standard *tempura* food is shrimp, or prawns, but all sorts of other foods are used.

(Ebi) Kakiage	*Tempura* leek and shrimp (chopped)
Ika kakiage	*Tempura* squid (chopped)
(Kisetsu) Yasai moriawase	Assortment of (seasonal) vegetable *tempura*
Tempura moriawase	Chef's selection of *tempura* pieces
Tendon	*Tempura* shrimp on rice

Soba and Udon

(Buckwheat and white flour noodles)

SOBA NOODLES ARE MADE from buckwheat (which is not actually wheat at all, but a berry) and are extremely popular in Japan. *Soba* can be either *kake-soba* or *mori-soba*. *Kake-soba* are served in a broth with a specific garnish, whereas *mori-soba* are served drained and cold and are dipped in a cold broth with *wasabi* and scallions. *Udon* noodles are made from wheat and are served hot like *kake-soba*, or cold like *mori-soba*. In Japan, there are specialty restaurants that serve *soba*, and generally *udon* as well. They range from little more than lunch counters to quite formal places, but they all tend to be inexpensive. In America, *soba* and *udon* dishes are generally offered at regular Japanese restaurants.

NOTE Both *soba* and *udon* noodles should be slurped when eaten, which allows you to eat them while they're still good and hot. If you're lucky enough to be at a Japanese restaurant on New Year's Eve, you'll undoubtedly be served *soba*, which represents a long life.

STYLES OF HOT *UDON* OR *SOBA* IN BROTH

Ankake	A thick, sweet mixture of fish, bamboo shoots, mushrooms, and wheat cakes
Chikara	Rice cakes (*mochi*)
Gomoku	Vegetables, egg, fish cakes, pork, and ham ("five ingredients")
Kake	Either *soba* or *udon* noodles in hot broth
Kakitama	Noodles with an egg
Kamo nanban	Scallions and wild duck

Kare nanban	Curried scallions
Kenchin	Taro, pork, and burdock root
Kitsune	Fried *tofu*
Nabeyaki udon	*Udon* noodles with vegetables, mushrooms, and eggs; sometimes served with *tempura* shrimp
Nameko	Small mushrooms
Natto	Fermented soybean paste
Niku nanban	Scallions and pork
Nishi	Herring
Okame	Fish cakes, mushrooms, bamboo shoots, and wheat cakes arranged over noodles
Okame toji	Eggs, fish cakes, bamboo shoots, mushrooms, and wheat cakes
Oroshi	Grated *daikon* (Japanese radish)
Oyako nanban	Parent and child, i.e. chicken and egg, with scallions
Sansai	Wild vegetables from the hills
Sukiyaki udon	*Udon* noodles with *sukiyaki*
Sutamina	*Mochi* and eggs
Tamago toji	Cooked egg and fish cake
Tanuki	*Tempura* batter
Tempura soba	*Tempura* shrimp
Ten nanban	*Tempura* shrimp and leeks
Ten toji	Egg and *tempura* shrimp

Tsukimi	Raw egg and dried seaweed
Wakame	Seaweed
Yamakake or *tororo*	Grated yam sauce
Zoni	Pounded rice cakes (*mochi*) with vegetables

COLD *SOBA* NOODLES

Hiyashi kitsune	Fried *tofu* with cold noodles
Hiyashi tanuki	Pieces of *tempura* batter with cold noodles
Mori	Cold *soba* noodles in a pile
Seiro	Either *zaru* or *mori*, depending on the establishment
Ten zaru	*Tempura* shrimp with cold *zaru soba*
Zaru	Dried seaweed strips

Tonkatsu (Pork cutlets)

TONKATSU IS sliced pork tenderloin that is breaded and deep-fried. But the definition hardly does justice to the juiciness, crunchy-tender texture, and delicious flavor of this simple fare. *Tonkatsu* restaurants are the most popular type of restaurant in Japan. Although the feature is obviously pork cutlets, other deep-fried foods are available in the *tonkatsu* restaurant, such as potato croquettes, chicken, and fish.

Chikin katsu	Batter-fried chicken cutlet
Chizu katsu	Deep-fried pork with cheese
Ebi furai	Fried shrimp
Hire katsu	Lean pork cutlet
Kaki furai	Fried oysters
Katsu ju	Pork cutlet over rice
Katsu sando	Pork cutlet sandwich
Korokke	Croquette, either crab or potato
Kushi katsu	Pork chunks on skewers with leeks
Menchi katsu	Ground beef patty, deep-fried
Mikkusu furai	An assortment of fried foods, such as shrimp, pork, and croquettes
Rosu katsu	Deep-fried pork cutlet with the fatty portion included
Tori kara-age	Deep-fried chicken without batter

Kushiage (Skewered foods)

SIMILAR TO *TONKATSU*, *kushiage* is simply another way to deep-fry various foods. The same delicious, crunchy bread coating covers tender morsels of food, but it is not pork, and it is served on skewers. Just about anything can be cooked this way, and the usual non-greasy, delicate flavor prevails. In Japan, specialty *kushiage* restaurants exist. They tend to be informal, almost pub-like places. *Kushiage* is also often available at *tonkatsu* restaurants and pubs.

The most common items fried for *kushiage* include seafood, especially shrimp, scallops, and squid, and all sorts of vegetables, especially *shiitake* mushrooms. *Kushiage* is a popular accompaniment to drinking alcohol, itself very popular in Japan.

—bekon-maki	Wrapped in bacon
Chizu	Cheese
Ebi	Shrimp
Geso	Squid tentacles
Gyu niku	Beef
Hasu	Lotus root
Hotategai	Scallops
Ika	Squid
Kisu	Smelt
Konnyaku	Devil's tongue, a type of gelatinous paste made from this plant
Kushi	Sticks
Kushiage kosu	An assortment of skewers
Okura	Okra
Sasami-maki	Rolled boneless chicken breast
—shiso-maki	Wrapped in *shiso* leaf
Uinna	Cocktail franks
Uzura	Quail eggs

Yakitori (Grilled chicken)

GRILLING IS AN age-old cooking technique in Japan. Like all other Japanese specialties, *yakitori* reaches a stage of perfection not seen in the food of many other cultures. Much of its appeal lies in its utter simplicity.

All *yakitori* food is served on skewers. Many parts of the chicken are used, including the skin and the organs. Sparrows, including the head, are popular in Japan. If you see something suspicious, you'd better ask what you're about to eat!

In addition to the chicken (or sparrow), many vegetables are often included on the skewer, such as *shiitake* mushrooms, peppers, *negi* (leeks), quail eggs, and gingko nuts.

Before grilling, the skewers are either seasoned with *tare* (basting sauce) or sprinkled with salt. That's it. The variable is the quality of the *tare* or the chef's touch with the salt. It's simple, but not easy. When you eat *yakitori*, you can sprinkle it with *shichimi*, a mixture of seven spices (usually white sesame seeds, black sesame seeds, *nori*, chili pepper, poppy seeds, *sansho* [hot red pepper], and orange peel).

Yakitori is especially popular as a bar-type food, much like chicken wings in American bars. Beer is the normal accompaniment. If you visit a Japanese restaurant that features *yakitori*, you're in for a great time with basic, tasty fare.

Hasami	Chicken and leek alternating on the skewer
Hone tsuki	With bones

Negima	Chicken and *negi*
Shio-aji	Salted (salt-style)
Tare-aji	Basted in sauce (*tare*-style)
Tori kimo yaki	Grilled chicken giblets
Tsukune	Chicken meatballs
Yakitori	Grilled, skewered chicken pieces
Yasai yaki	Vegetables grilled on a skewer

Kamameshi (Specialty rice dishes)

A KAMA IS A SMALL POT, *meshi* is rice, but *kamameshi* is a lot more than just rice cooked in a pot. There are endless varieties of this meal-in-a-pot marvel. Created in the 19th century, *kamameshi* can be any combination of shrimp, *shiitake* mushrooms, chicken, bamboo shoots, oysters, scallops, fish, crab, and chopped vegetables steamed with rice. The primary seasoning is soy sauce. *Kamameshi* is a popular dish for *ekiben* and is also served frequently with *yakitori*.

Asari	Clams
Awabi	Abalone
Ebi	Cooked shrimp
Gomoku	A mixture of fried *tofu*, chicken, seafood, mushrooms, and vegetables
Gyu	Beef
Hotategai	Scallops

Kaki	Oysters
Kani	Crabmeat
Kuri	Chestnuts
Matsutake	Pine mushrooms
Sake	Salmon
Sansai	Assorted vegetables from the hills
Sanshoku	Boiled egg, vegetables, and crumbled pink cod meat
Takenoko	Bamboo shoots
Tori	Chicken

Nabemono, Sukiyaki, and Shabu-Shabu

A *nabe* is a cooking pot, and *nabemono* is cooked at the table. The style of cooking is informal—everyone cooks the dish together and eats from the same pot. A pot of boiling broth is at the table on a gas burner, then the various ingredients are dumped in according to how long they take to cook.

The famous special type of *nabemono* is beef *sukiyaki*, which is made not by the customer but the staff. *Sukiyaki* starts with each person sautéing the thin slices of beef, then adding broth and vegetables. When it's done, everyone reaches into the communal pot with chopsticks, takes a morsel of food, and dips it into a raw egg that each person has in a small dish. The barely mixed egg is the only part that takes some getting used to, but it really does enhance the taste and texture of the food. Plus, the food slides down your throat better.

Shabu-shabu is yet another variation, in which the customer dips meat and vegetables into broth to cook them. This is similar to meat fondue, but uses broth rather than hot oil.

Anko-nabe	Anglerfish *nabemono*
Chanko-nabe	*Nabemono* intended to fatten *sumo* wrestlers. Traditionally, no four-legged animals are used, as defeat is signified by being on all fours. Common ingredients include chicken, *negi*, fish, and vegetables.
Chiri-nabe	Fish and vegetable *nabemono*
Dote-nabe	Oyster *nabemono* with *miso*
Hire sukiyaki	Beef tenderloin *sukiyaki*
Kaki-nabe	Vegetable and oyster *nabemono*
Kamo-nabe	Duck *nabemono*
Matsuzaka gyu	*Matsuzaka* beef
Mizutaki	Chicken *nabemono*; it's dipped in *ponzu* as you eat it
Ponzu	A dipping sauce made from citrus fruits and soy sauce

Rosu sukiyaki	*Sukiyaki* with regular beef
Shabu-shabu	Thinly sliced beef cooked quickly in broth
Shimofuri sukiyaki	*Sukiyaki* with special-grade beef
Sukiyaki	Thinly sliced beef and vegetables
Tara-nabe	Codfish stew with vegetables
Udon-suki	Fish *nabemono* with *udon*
Yanagawa-nabe	*Nabemono* of loach (a small eel), egg, and burdock root
Yose-nabe	Vegetable *nabemono* with either chicken or seafood
Yudofu	Boiled *tofu*

NOTE The famous *Kobe* beef comes from animals that are fed a special diet and are massaged to keep the muscles soft. It's very tasty and tender because of a lot of marbling (fat). It's also very expensive.

Oden (Fish-dumpling stew)

IN JAPAN, ODEN STALLS crop up as the weather cools, and Japan's most casual dining of all keeps people nourished throughout the colder seasons. *Oden* can be any of several types of fish dumplings in a stew with various vegetables. Subtle in flavor, it's very inexpensive and popular.

Chikuwa	Sausage-shaped fish mixture
Chikuwa-bu	Sausage-shaped wheat gluten cake
Gobo-maki	Fish cake with burdock root
Hanpen	Fish-paste cake, made with yam
Ika-maki	Baby squid in a fish cake
Konnyaku	Devil's-tongue starch made into blocks. They can be cubed or sliced, and are used in *oden* for texture, which in this case is chewy.
Roru kyabetsu	Cabbage rolls stuffed with sausage or burdock
Satsuma-age	Fried fish cakes
Tsumire	Fish balls

Miso (Soy and grain paste)

MISO IS A FERMENTED PASTE made from soybeans with other grains often added. It is used as the base for *miso* soup, a nutritious mainstay of Japanese cuisine. It's also used in various dishes as a flavoring.

Akadashi	Red *miso* soup
Miso shiru	*Miso* soup (any of various blends of soy paste)
Nameko-jiru	*Miso* soup with tiny mushrooms
Ton-jiru	*Miso* soup with pork and vegetables

Side Dishes and Miscellaneous Foods

Aburage	Fried *tofu*
Aemono	Cooked salad, dressed with various sauces
Agedashidofu	Fried *tofu* topped with condiments, in a broth
Agedofu	Thick-sliced *tofu* used in various preparations
Akadashi	Soup made with brown *miso*
Atsuage	Fried blocks of *tofu*
Bata	Butter
Bifun	Thin rice noodles
Chahan	Fried rice
Chawan	Rice bowl
Chawan mushi	A custard with chicken and vegetables
Chazuke	Rice with vegetables added and green tea poured over it
Chizu	Cheese
Chokoreto	Chocolate
Daifuku	A Japanese rice cake filled with sweet bean jam
Dango	Dumplings
Datemaki	A rolled omelette
Dengaku	Foods broiled on a skewer with sweetened *miso*
Fu	Wheat gluten

Fukujinzuke	A pickled mixture of seven vegetables served with Japanese curry
Ganmodoki	Fried balls of *tofu* and various mixed vegetables
Gomoku	A variety of ingredients added to a dish
Harusame	Very thin, "spring rain" noodles made from mung bean, potato, or sweet potato starch
Hayashi raisu	Beef and onion over rice
Hitashi	Cooked greens seasoned with bonito flakes and soy sauce
Hiyayakko	Cold *tofu* with Welsh onions and seasonings
Ishikarinabe	Hokkaido-style salmon stew
Isobemaki	Grilled *mochi* in seaweed
Kakiage	Diced shrimp, *tempura* style
Kamaboko	Fish loaf that is sliced and used in soup or stew
Kani zosui	Rice soup with crabmeat
Katsu don	Pork and vegetables over rice
Kijiju / Kijidon	Grilled chicken over rice
Kinpira	A burdock stew with carrots, soy sauce, and spices
Kishimen	Flat wheat noodles

Konnyaku	A gelatinous paste made from devil's tongue, formed into blocks, then sliced or broken up into other dishes
Mabodofu	A spicy dish of meat and *tofu*
Manju	A sweet bun with either sweet or savory filling
Miruku/Gyu nyu	Milk
Mochi	Rice cakes. Glutinous rice that is cooked and pounded into a paste, then formed into cakes. They are soft if eaten this way. If left to dry, they get hard and are then toasted. *Mochi* are an essential part of daily Japanese fare.
Nama yasai	Raw vegetables
Nerimono	Fish paste products
Okayu	Rice porridge
Okazu	Side dish
Okonomiyaki	Japanese pancakes, made from eggs, often called "Japanese pizza." It's a very popular dish in Japan. Any number of ingredients can be included (such as pork, squid, shrimp, or beef),

and in some cases the customer makes his or her own on a grill. The batter is a flour-and-egg combination, and turning the pancake requires some skill.

Omuretsu	Omelette
Otsumami	Hors d'oeuvre eaten while drinking alcohol
Oyakodon	Chicken and eggs over rice
Panko	Bread crumbs
Potaju	Potage
Purin	Egg custard
Ramen	Chinese egg noodles that are extremely popular and widely available in Japan, usually served in a broth with slices of pork and vegetables
Sekihan	Steamed glutinous rice with *azuki* (adzuki beans)
Senbei	Rice cracker
Shinko	Pickled cucumber, radish, eggplant, and cabbage
Shirataki	Translucent noodles make from *konnyaku;* a standard ingredient in *sukiyaki*

Shumai	Chinese-style pork dumplings (*dim sum*)
Soba	Buckwheat noodles
Somen	Very thin wheat noodles
Sunomono	Salad with vinegar; may consist of seafood and/or vegetables
Takuan	Pickled *daikon*, the most common of Japanese pickles
Tamago zosui	Rice soup with egg
Tenshindon	Rice with crab and egg
Tori zosui	Rice soup with chicken
Tsukemono	Pickled vegetables. All sorts of pickles are served in Japanese cuisine.
Tsukudani	Seafood and various vegetables preserved by being cooked in soy sauce, *mirin*, and sugar until almost dry. Used as a garnish, especially in rice dishes.
Tsumire	Fish balls
Udon	Thick wheat noodles
Uzura no tamago	Quail eggs
Yudofu	*Tofu* simmered in water
Zasai	Chinese pickle
Zosui	Rice gruel with fish and vegetables

Desserts

In Japan, dessert is not eaten after meals, so restaurants there don't serve it. Sweets are fairly limited in scope, although Western-style desserts and sweets are readily available in Japan. Desserts are found at home and in *kammi-dokoro* (sweet shops). Gelatin desserts are very common, made with agar-agar rather than with animal-based gelatin. Rice is another common ingredient.

Aisu	Ice cream
An	Sweet red bean paste
Anmitsu	Gelatin with *an,* oranges, and dark syrup
Furutsu anmitsu	*Anmitsu* with mixed fruit
Kuri anmitsu	*Anmitsu* with chestnuts
Kurimu anmitsu	*Anmitsu* topped with ice cream
Kuzukiri	Pudding made from *kudzu* starch, served with dark syrup
Mitarashi dango	*Mochi* balls with sweet soy sauce
Mitsumame	Gelatin with oranges and dark syrup
Shiruko	Sweet soup served warm, made with *an* and *mochi*
Zenzai	A soup much like *shiruko* but chunkier

Alcoholic Beverages

Alcohol is very popular in Japan. In fact, it is rude to decline a drink. If you don't want a drink, an appropriate response is to cite a medical reason for not being able to drink. The most popular drink by far is beer, followed by *sake*. Businesspeople also drink whiskey, generally Scotch or bourbon. In Japanese restaurants in the United States, patrons often choose *sake* in order to have a Japanese experience.

NOTE In Japan, you always allow someone else to fill your glass, and you should fill other people's glasses. Never fill your own.

Drunkenness is fairly common in Japan; it seems to serve as a release from the strict behavior codes that govern business and other daytime activities. Silly behavior is expected, and men often will act drunker than they really are. The next day, though, no one talks about the night before. Everything returns to normal.

SAKE

Sake is distilled from rice and is usually fortified with alcohol. It ranges from sweet to dry and is served either warm or cold. Whereas Japanese won't drink *sake* throughout the meal, Americans will, and it's perfectly okay to do so in the

United States. After all, restaurateurs don't want to discourage sales.

Other than by studying the fairly complex art of making *sake*, the best way to learn about it is just to drink it. Ask the server for a recommendation. As you drink different types, you can compare and contrast and develop your own list of favorites. Be careful, especially with warm *sake*, because it's smooth and therefore easy to drink too much.

NOTE In Japan, it's okay to drink during the meal, but you should finish *sake* before rice is served. *Sake* and rice are absolutely never served together.

Aka wain	Red wine
Babon	Bourbon
Biru	Beer
Chuhai	A mixed drink made with *shochu*
Gurasu wain	Glass of wine
Jin	Gin
Jin tonikku	Gin and tonic
Jinja eru	Ginger ale
Jusu	Juice or soft drink
Kora	Cola
Kori	Ice
Kuro nama biru	Dark draft beer

Matini	Martini; as in most of the world, this refers in Japan to vermouth (after Martini and Rossi vermouth). You have to specify sweet or dry. If you want gin in your martini, order gin with ice.
Mizuwari	Whiskey and water
Nama biru	Draft beer
Nihon-shu	Japanese wine; *sake*
Orenji	Orange drink
Raimu sawa	Lime sour
Remon sawa	Lemon sour
Sake	*Sake*, Japanese rice wine
Sawa	A sour made from *shochu*
Shiro wain	White wine
Shochu	Japanese grain liquor that resembles vodka
Sodawari	Scotch and soda
Sukotchi	Scotch
Tansan	Club soda
Tonikku uota	Tonic water
Uisuki	Whiskey
Ume sawa	Plum sour
Uokka	Vodka
Uron sawa	*Shochu* and *oolong* tea
Wain	Wine

Tea and Coffee

Both beverages are popular in Japan, although Japanese restaurants in the United States don't offer the wide range of coffee drinks available in Japanese coffee shops.

Aisu kohi	Iced coffee (extremely popular in Japan)
Amerikan	American-style coffee, quite weak
Kocha	Tea (black tea)
Kohi	Coffee
O-cha	"Green" tea. The best and most expensive is *gyokuro*. Next is *sencha*, and everyday tea is *bancha*.

THE TEA CEREMONY

Tea holds an almost sacred place in Japanese society. Enjoyed for its spiritual nature, tea's stature has solidified through the centuries. It's no wonder, then, that the formal tea ceremony is so venerated today.

Originating from rules established by the samurai in the 14th century, the tea ceremony of today, called *chanoyu,* was formalized in the 16th century by tea master Sen no Rikyu. Essentially, the tea ceremony is an aesthetic pursuit in which the guests savor tea while they contemplate the beauty of their surroundings—beautiful tea implements, works of art, flowers, and meticulous landscaping.

Generally, there are up to four guests, and the event is held in a room designed just for tea ceremonies. A special powdered green tea, *matcha,* is used, and there are strict rules for brewing the tea, as well as for every aspect of the ceremony. The tea ceremony, reflecting its Zen influence, attempts to lift the guests from the coarse material world into an ethereal state of meditation. This is no ordinary quaffing.

If all this sounds like a highly stylized, formal rite with inflexible rules, you have the right idea. Some simple guidelines, should you be lucky enough to receive an invitation to a tea ceremony, are to arrive on time, remove your shoes, drink all your tea, and eat all your food. Also, be sure to study the tea implements and other lovely artifacts, and compliment the host. You will then have a most enjoyable experience and be a good guest at the same time.

Glossary

MEATS	
Aigamo	Duck
Baniku	Horse meat
Bonchiri	Chicken tail
Butaniku	Pork
Chikin	Chicken
Gyuniku	Beef
Hamu	Ham
Hanbaga	Hamburger
Hanbagu	Hamburger steak
Hatsu	Heart
Hina	Very young chicken
Kamo	Wild duck
Kawa	Chicken skin
Kohitsuji	Lamb
Kon bifu	Corned beef
Koushi	Veal
Kujira	Whale
Momo	Chicken leg
Motsu	Giblets
Nankotsu	Bone-in chicken
Poku	Pork
Reba	Chicken liver
Sasami	Chicken breast
Shichimencho	Turkey

Shika	Venison
Shoniku	Meat with skin
Sunagimo	Gizzards
Suteki	Steak
Suzume	Sparrow, including its bones and head. The head should be crunched for special appreciation. Not a common item in American-Japanese restaurants. Save this delightful experience for your next trip to Japan.
Tan	Beef tongue
Tebasaki	Chicken wing
Tori	Chicken
Tsukune	Chicken meatballs
Uinna	Vienna sausage or wiener
Uzura	Quail
Wakadori	Young chicken

SEAFOOD

Ainame	Rock trout
Aji	Horse mackerel
Amadai	Red tilefish
Anago	Conger eel
Anko	Anglerfish
Aoyagi	Round clam
Asari	Littleneck clam

Awabi	Abalone
Ayu	Sweet fish
Dojo	Loach, a small eel
Ebi	Shrimp
Ei	Skate or ray
Fugu	Blowfish
Fuka	Shark
Geso	Squid tentacles
Ginpo	Gunnel
Gyokai	Seafood
Hamaguri	Clam
Haze	Goby
Himono	Dried seafood
Hirame	Flounder, sole
Hire	Fillet
Hokke	Atka mackerel
Hotategai	Scallops
Iidako	Small octopus
Ika	Squid
Iseebi	Spiny lobster
Kai	Shellfish
Kaibashira	Valve muscle of a mollusk
Kaki	Oyster
Kani	Crab
Katsuo	Bonito
Kisu	Sillago

Koebi	Small shrimp
Kuruma-ebi	Prawn
Maguro	Tuna
Megochi	Flathead
Mirugai	Surf clam
Mutsu	Bluefish
Nishin	Herring
Saba	Mackerel
Sakana	Fish
Sake	Salmon
Sawara	Spanish mackerel
Shako	Mantis shrimp
Shiba-ebi	Prawn
Shirauo	Whitebait
Shishamo	Smelt
Suzuki	Sea bass
Taishoebi	Prawn or shrimp
Tako	Octopus
Tara	Cod
Torigai	Cockle
Tsumire	Fish cake
Tsuna	Canned tuna
Wakasagi	Smelt (freshwater)
Yamame	Brown trout

VEGETABLES, GRAINS, AND OTHER PLANT PRODUCTS

Amaguri	Roasted chestnuts
Anzu	Apricot
Asatsuki	Chives
Asupara	Asparagus
Azuki	Adzuki beans
Banana	Banana
Biwa	Loquat
Budo	Grapes
Burokkori	Broccoli
Daidai	Bitter orange
Daikon	Japanese radish
Daizu	Soybeans
Edamame	Green soybeans
Endo	Peas
Enoki	Thin white mushrooms
Fuki no to	Coltsfoot buds
Furutsu	Fruit
Genmai	Brown rice
Ginnan	Gingko nuts
Gobo	Burdock root
Gohan	Rice
Goma	Sesame seeds
Gurepufurutsu	Grapefruit
Hakumai	White rice
Hakusai	Bok choy

Hasu	Lotus root
Hijiki	Brown algae
Horenso	Spinach
Hoshibudo	Raisins
Ichigo	Strawberry
Ichijiku	Fig
Imo	Potato
Ingen	Green beans
Jagaimo	White potato
Kabocha	Pumpkin, squash
Kabu	White turnip
Kaiso	Seaweed
Kaiware	*Daikon* shoots
Kaki	Persimmon
Karifurawa	Cauliflower
Kiichigo	Raspberry
Kikuna	Chrysanthemum (edible)
Kikurage	Tree ear (fungus)
Kinako	Soybean flour
Kinoko	Mushroom
Kinome	Prickly ash leaves
Kohi	Coffee
Kokoa	Cocoa
Kokonattsu	Coconut
Kokumotsu	Grain
Komen	Uncooked rice
Komugiko	Wheat flour

Kon	Corn
Konbu	Kelp
Konnyaku	Block of devil's-tongue starch
Kudamono	Fruit
Kuri	Chestnut
Kurumi	Walnut
Kuwai	Water chestnut
Kuzu	*Kudzu* or its starch
Kyabetsu	Cabbage
Kyuri	Cucumber
Mame	Bean
Mango	Mango
Masukatto	Muscat grapes
Matsutake	Pine mushroom, a rare find in Japan, highly prized for its exquisite flavor, and very expensive. Many are imported from Korea.
Mekyabetsu	Brussels sprouts
Meron	Melon
Meshi	Cooked rice
Mikan	Mandarin orange
Mitsuba	Trefoil leaf
Momo	Peach
Moyashi	Bean sprouts
Mugi	Wheat

Myoga	A type of ginger, although only the buds and stems are used. They're pickled and used as garnishes.
Naganegi	Leek
Nameko	Very small mushrooms
Nashi	Japanese pear
Nasu	Eggplant
Negi	Welsh onion, much like a leek but longer and thinner, found here in Asian markets
Ninjin	Carrot
Ninniku	Garlic
Ninniku no me	Garlic stems
Nira	Chives
Nori	Dried seaweed, used for rolling *sushi*
Nuka	Rice bran
Okara	The outside (bran) of the soybean; very nutritious, but not very pleasing on the palate
Okura	Okra
Painappuru	Pineapple
Papaiya	Papaya
Paseri	Parsley
Piman	Green pepper
Poteto	Potato
Puramu	Plum

Purun	Prune
Raichi	Litchi
Raimu	Lime
Raisu	Rice
Rakkyo	A type of scallion with a strong flavor, usually pickled
Reishi	Litchi
Remon	Lemon
Renkon	Lotus root
Retasu	Lettuce
Ringo	Apple
Sakuranbo	Cherry
Sasage	Black-eyed peas
Satoimo	Taro
Satsumaimo	Sweet potato
Sayaendo	Snow peas
Serori	Celery
Shiitake	Japanese mushrooms (also known as Chinese black mushrooms; in the past, they were available only dried); they are now cultivated and easy to find
Shishito	Small green pepper
Shiso	Perilla leaves. There are two kinds, red and green. Red (*akajiso*) are used primarily for color. Green

	(*aojiso*) are similar to mint or basil. The buds are also used.
Shoga	Ginger
Shungiku	Chrysanthemum leaves
Soramame	Fava bean
Sudachi	Type of lemon
Takenoko	Bamboo shoots
Tamanegi	Onion
Tara no me	Buds of Hercules'-club tree
Tofu	Bean curd made from soybean milk derived from boiling soybeans. *Tofu* has a custard-like texture and is high in protein. Japanese take *tofu* making very seriously, and the finest Japanese *tofu* has a wonderfully smooth texture. Its bland taste and soft-yet-firm texture make *tofu* extremely versatile.
Tomorokoshi	Corn
Tonyu	Soy milk
Tororo	Grated yam
Ume	Japanese green plum
Warabi	Mountain bracken, used in soup
Wasabi	Japanese green horseradish
Yamaimo	Japanese yam

Yasai	Vegetables
Yashinomi	Coconut
Yonashi	Pear
Yurine	Lily bulb
Yuzu	Citron
Zakuro	Pomegranate
Zenmai	The royal fern, similar to *warabi*; its unopened fronds are fiddleheads

SAUCES AND CONDIMENTS

Abura	Oil
An	Sweet paste made from *azuki*
Banira	Vanilla
Chomi ryo	Seasonings
Denbu	Pink fish paste
Gari	Sliced ginger macerated in rice-wine vinegar, used as a condiment with *sushi*
Goma-shio	Sesame seeds mixed with salt
Hachimitsu	Honey
Ichimi	Powdered red pepper
Karakuchi-sosu	Sauce very much like Worcestershire
Karashi	Japanese mustard
Katsuobushi	Dried, cured, smoked bonito flakes. This product is used a great deal, providing the base for *dashi* as

well as a seasoning in a large number of dishes. The dried bonito resembles a piece of wood, and it's shaved before it is used. Although few people shave it to order, that is considered the best way to use *katsuobushi*, as much of its flavor is so volatile.

Kechappu	Ketchup
Koshinryo	Spices
Kosho	Black pepper
Makuchi-sosu	Thick, sweet sauce
Ponzu	Citrus juices, or citrus juices with soy sauce and/or vinegar
Sato	Sugar
Sosu	Sauce
Togarashi	(Hot) red pepper

MISCELLANEOUS CULINARY TERMS

-age	Fried
Aji	Taste
Ama	Sweet
Amiyaki	Cooked over a wire grill
Asa gohan	Breakfast
Bento	Boxed lunch. Very popular in Japan. People put all sorts of foods in these boxes. Rice is invariably

included, as are a selection of those foods that taste good cold or at room temperature. A great concept for people on the go.

Chukafu	Chinese style
Guratan	Au gratin
Hashi	Chopsticks
Hiyamugi	Thin white noodles, served in cold water
Hiyashi	Cold
Hiyashi-	Cold noodles with whatever garnish follows
Horokuyaki	Baked with salt in a covered dish
-iri	Stuffed with
Itamae	Chef, especially a *sushi* chef
-itame	Stir-fried
Kare	Curry
Kosu	Full-course meal
Menyu	Menu
Miso-	With *miso* sauce
Mizu	Water
Moriawase	Assorted platter
Naifu	Knife
Nami	Regular size
-nanban	With leek
Nori-	Dried seaweed
O-	Large portion

Omakase	Chef's choice
Omori	Large size
Oyako	Parent and child (chicken and egg)
Raisu	Plain white rice
Ranchi	Lunch
Ryori	Cuisine
Sake-	Salmon
Somen	Very thin white noodles
Susume	Special of the day
Tarako-	Cod roe
Teishoku	A complete meal, usually with rice, pickles, and soup
Ten-	With *tempura* shrimp
-toji	With egg
Tori-	Very rare chicken
-tsuki	Including
Ume-	Japanese plum
Yoshoku	Japanese-style Western dishes
-zen	Full-course meal

Pan-Asian Cuisine
Laos
Cambodia
Malaysia
Indonesia

SOUTHEAST ASIAN CUISINE IS gaining more and more popularity in the United States. American diners, always looking for new flavor sensations, enjoy Asian cuisines not only for their great taste, but for their perceived healthful qualities. Therefore, in addition to the sections of the book devoted to Thai, Vietnamese, Japanese, and Korean cuisines, the Pan-Asian section will take you on a culinary journey to some up-and-coming culinary stars. There are some truly delicious foods that will inspire you to explore the cuisines even further on your own.

Lao Cuisine

What Makes it Lao: Special Ingredients in Lao Cuisine

LAOS SHARES MANY FOODS with its Indo-Chinese neighbors. Stir-fries and curries are common, and lots of the condiments and vegetables used in Lao cuisine are those found throughout Southeast Asia. There are strong culinary influences in Laos from Thailand, India, and Malaysia, as well as from China.

Fish is extremely important to Lao cuisine. Indeed, fish—almost always freshwater fish—is the single most important protein source in Laos. The mighty Mekong River, after all, is the border between Laos and Thailand. Fish is often eaten raw, but other cooking procedures are used as well. Many species of fish are used, most of which don't exist in the United States. It's common for Lao restaurants in America to use many of the less-expensive varieties of fish not much utilized by American and European restaurants. It's an economical way to give a Lao touch to fish dishes.

A great deal of water buffalo is eaten in Laos. So is beef, its expensive substitute. In the United States, of course, Lao restaurants use beef. Pork is also very popular, and three-layer pork—skin, fat, and lean as one slab—is a staple of the Lao kitchen. Chicken and other poultry are enjoyed, but in Laos they're more expensive than pork.

In Laos, like in other Southeast Asian countries, the cook considers rice to be the main part of the meal and the other dishes as condiments or small accompaniments. Lao cuisine is the only one in Southeast Asia to use glutinous or sticky rice in most meals. In other countries, sticky rice is reserved for sweet dishes. Traditionally, Laos eat with their hands, often grabbing a bit of sticky rice and using it to pick up messier foods or to mop up sauces. Outside influences have changed this method somewhat, but it's still considered the authentic eating style. Chopsticks are used for eating noodles from soup, but that's it.

The most common seasonings are chilies, garlic, gin-

ger, mint, turmeric, lemongrass, shallots, and the ubiquitous *narm pa,* or fish sauce, spring onions, and other herbs
that are uncommon and not available in the United States.
Fried onions, shallots, and garlic are typical and common
garnishes, as are chopped scallions. Lao cuisine includes lots
of greens, many of them unfamiliar to Americans. As Southeast Asian cuisines become more popular, though, more of
their greens and other produce are showing up in American
markets.

DORK KHIING
Ginger flowers, delicately aromatic.

LAAP
People in Laos have been eating their version of steak
tartare for many generations. In fact, they eat a great deal of
their meats and fish raw. *Laap* is traditionally raw or half-
cooked beef or water buffalo meat that is pounded into a
puree together with cow liver and strife. It is seasoned with
khar (galanga root), lemon, *pa daek* (fermented fish sauce),
salt, roasted rice, chilies, spring onion, scallions, and mint.
Standard Lao seasonings are also used—*narm pa*, scallions,
mint, and lime juice. Other preparations using fish or other
meats are also common, and the name of the ingredient fol-
lows the word *"laap."* For example, *laap pa keung* is minced
and seasoned raw *pa keung*, a Lao fish. It is sometimes served
with lettuce leaves for wrapping and a spicy sauce for dip-

ping. Although *laap* is always finely chopped and pounded, it can be partly cooked.

MARK PII

Male buds of banana flowers.

PA DAEK

Fish sauce with chunks of fermented fish, rice husks, and rice dust. It sounds a bit much, and its smell can knock you down, but as a seasoning it works in subtle undertones.

SOMMUU

A pickled pork sausage, *sommuu* is one of the most popular foods of Laos. It is extremely spicy and takes a certain amount of palate training for many Americans!

Typical Dishes

As in other Southeast Asian countries, the Lao meal is typically served all at once. Soup is always served, either with the meal or at the end, but never as a starter. Like Vietnam, Lao cuisine exhibits remnants of French influence in its French bread, European-style roasted meats, potatoes, wine, coffee, and pastries. These aren't part of the traditional foods, of course, but most Laos eat them regularly. Chinese influence over the cuisine is also very strong, and there is the residual influence of Indian immigration as well. Although people from Laos and Thailand are ethnically the same, their cuisines have evolved with their own styles.

It is very difficult to find a Lao restaurant in the United States that serves only Lao cuisine. Instead, restaurants offer a great assortment of dishes with Chinese and Thai roots, and with other influences as well. The little touches make it Lao, but don't expect pure Lao dishes.

KAENG JEUUD KALAMPI
Cabbage and pork soup with eggs. added as if for egg drop soup.

KAENG KAI SAI HED
Chicken soup with mushrooms.

KAENG LONE KAI
Chicken soup with vermicelli, typically seasoned, and garnished with squid, sliced omelette, native mushrooms, cilantro, and chopped scallions.

KAENG PA SAY
Clear fish soup, made with a pork stock and garnished with vermicelli, scallions, cilantro, and thinly sliced omelette.

KAENG PHAAK KARD MEO

A soup of the Meo (Hmong) people made from Chinese mustard greens and pork stock.

KAENG ORM DUUK NGOUA

Beef soup with rice, seasoned with crushed ginger, lemongrass, and shallots.

KAENG SOM HOUA PA KEUNG

Barb (a native Lao fish similar to a rock bass) soup. Typical to Lao fish soups, the standard combination of lemongrass, *narm pa*, and scallions makes a light broth with a citrus accent.

KAENG SOM HOUA PA VA SAI HED LA NGOK

Fish soup made from the head of a *pa va* (freshwater fish) and *het la ngok* (orange mushroom). Typically seasoned with lemongrass, scallions, and *narm pa*.

KAENG SOM KALAMPI

Pork and cabbage soup with tomatoes, lemongrass, and *narm pa*, garnished with scallions.

KAENG SOM PA

A basic fish soup that includes lemongrass, cilantro, lime, *narm pa*, and diced tomatoes, it is *the* quintessential Lao fish soup.

KAI YAD SAI

Chicken stuffed with shallots, garlic, chilies, and cilantro, slowly braised and served in pieces surrounding the stuffing.

KALEE PED

Curried duck, made with coconut milk but has more of an Indian curry flavor than a Thai curry flavor; served with potatoes and garnished with cilantro.

KHOUA PAD KHIING KAI

Fried chicken braised with coconut milk, ginger, onions, and shallots, seasoned with *narm pa,* cilantro, and garlic.

KNAAP KUUNG

Chopped shrimp seasoned with lemongrass, shallots, chilies, and scallions, wrapped in a banana leaf and grilled.

KNAAP PA

Fish baked in banana skins with pork, lemongrass, chilies, shallots, and *narm pa.*

KNAAP PA YON

Banana leaves stuffed with catfish and seasoned with pork fat, *narm pa,* shallots, basil, and chilies.

MOWK PA

Steamed catfish, usually in a banana leaf, seasoned in the typical way with *narm pa*, lemongrass, shallots, cilantro, and chilies.

MOWK SOM PA

Pickled fish roe wrapped in banana leaves and grilled. The mixture is seasoned with a typical assortment of lemongrass, scallions, shallots, garlic, chilies, and cilantro.

NIENE MAAK KHEUA

Stir-fried fish and eggplant paste with bean sprouts and scallions, seasoned with garlic, shallots, and *narm pa*.

ORW LARM NOK KHO

Quail stew, quite strongly seasoned with *padek* and chilies. Dried quail is used, which has a very strong flavor as well. Typical vegetables would be Asian round eggplants, scallions, and greens.

ORW SOD HUA PA SA NGOUA

Fish head soup with young eggplants, mushrooms, greens, and chilies. While the fish called for is a type of sheatfish found in Laos, any firm-fleshed freshwater fish would be used in the United States. Farm-raised catfish or tilapia are common in many Southeast Asian restaurants. The market determines the fish used to a great extent.

ORW SOD KAI

Chicken stew with standard Lao seasonings, eggplants, and mushrooms.

PED HUM SAI HOUA PHAK PEUK

Duck stuffed with gizzards, liver, shallots, onions, and bread, braised and served with Chinese radishes, garnished with—you guessed it—cilantro. For duck lovers, this dish is absolutely delicious.

PED TOM KHATHI

Duck and galanga root soup with coconut milk. A rich and satisfying soup with a lot of galanga root and garlic zest.

SA SIN NGOUA

Beef marinated in lime juice and served with a mixture of garlic, lemongrass, shallots, chilies, and galanga root. The dish is garnished with boiled heart, liver, and tripe. This traditional dish is served with *kaeng orm duuk ngoua*, a lightly seasoned beef broth.

Glossary

MEATS	
Beef—*Siin ngoua*	
Beab vithi tad steak	Porterhouse steak
Hua chai	Heart
Siik khong kaduuk khaang	Rib
Siin orn	Tenderloin
Siin sanh	Fillet
Siin sanh nai ngoua	Sirloin
Siin steak	Steak
Steak siin khaang	Flank steak
Toon siin	Round
Tuub	Liver
Lamb—*Kae*	
Ba lai	Shoulder
Kaduuk khone	Rack
Kaeng	Shank
Siin kae	Mutton
Siin korn kae	Chop
Siin korn kudookang	Rib chop
Siin sanh	Loin, saddle
Siin sanh piang	Loin chop
Siin tom peua	Stew

Pork—*Muu*

Gio	Vietnamese sausage
Haem	Ham
Hiim sob	Lips
Ka duuk khang	Spareribs
Muu haem sod	Fresh ham
Muu kem ob khuan fai	Smoked ham
Nang muu	Pork skin
Piing duuk khang	Barbecued spareribs
Sai oua	Sausage
Sai oua wan	Chinese sausage
Siin kone	Loin
Siin korn muu khem	Bacon
Siin koteulat muu	Chop

Chicken—*Kai*

Kai mae	Hen
Kai phu tone	Capon
Kha	Leg
Kheuang nai	Giblets
Kok kha	Thigh
Na euk	Breast
Peek	Wings
Siin na euk kai	Boneless breast
Tai kai	Gizzard
Tone kha to	Drumstick

Tone siin koteulat	Cutlet
Tubb	Liver

Turkey—*Kai nguang*

Na euk	Breast
Siin cheun	Cutlet
Siin kai gnuang bod	Ground turkey

Veal—*Nang*

Kha	Leg
Khai lung	Kidneys
Khao jii waan	Sweetbreads
Na khaeng	Shank
Sanh laang	Loin
Siin euk	Breast
Siin ko teu let	Chop, cutlet
Siin peun	Shoulder
Tubb	Liver

Goat—*Bae*

Siin ko teu let	Chop
Siin sanh	Saddle

Poultry—*Sard piik*

Harn	Goose
Kai paa	Pheasant
Nork ka jork thaepp	Ostrich

Nork kang kae	Squab (pigeon)
Nork ka tha	Partridge
Nork khoom	Quail
Ped	Duck

Game—*Sard paa*

Ka tai	Rabbit
Khuai	Buffalo
Kouang, farne	Venison
Moo paa	Boar

SEAFOOD

Fin fish—*Khii pa*

Iian	Eel
Pa bass	Bass
Pa bluefish	Bluefish
Pa duuk	Catfish
Pa flounder	Flounder
Pa gnai khai ku pa salarm	Sturgeon
Pa grouper	Grouper
Pa herring	Herring
Pa ka thong dan lem	Swordfish
Pa khao	Whitefish
Pa kod	Cod
Pa lin ma	Sole

Pa monkfish	Monkfish
Pa perch khai ku pa niin	Perch
Pa phane tha lae	Turbot
Pa roughy	Orange roughy
Pa sa larm	Shark
Pa salmon	Salmon
Pa sardine	Sardine
Pa scrod	Scrod
Pa shad	Shad
Pa snapper daeng	Red snapper
Pa tha lae darm bass	Black sea bass
Pa tha lae haddock	Haddock
Pa tha lae mackerel	Holy mackerel
Pa tha lae tuna	Tuna
Pa thoo mackerel	Mackerel
Pa truite	Trout

Shellfish—*Sat narm pa pha pheuak hum*

Huoi abalone	Abalone
Huoi chub	Conch
Huoi kab	Clam, mussel
Huoi khaeng	Cockle
Hoai nang lom	Oyster
Hoai Saint Jacques	Scallop
Ka pu	Crab

PAN-ASIAN CUISINE

Kuung	Prawn
Kuung nam cheud	Crayfish
Kuung ngai	Lobster
Kuung noi	Shrimp
Pa eeheu	Squid
Pa meuk	Cuttlefish
Pa meuk ngark	Octopus

DAIRY PRODUCTS

Ka laem	Ice cream
Kheung neung	Half-and-half
Kreem	Cream
Kreem penh korn	Clotted cream
Kreem sod	Crème fraîche
Kreem som	Sour cream
Kreem tee	Whipped cream
Narm marn beur	Butter
Narm nom	Nonfat milk
Neui kuai	Ghee
Neui magarine	Margarine
Nom	Milk
Nom neui	Buttermilk
Nom sod	Clarified butter
Nom som	Yogurt
Nom thua pai	Whole milk

Khai	Egg

VEGETABLES

Cu dau	Jicama
Hark celery	Celery root
Hed	Mushroom
Hed dam	*Shiitake* or black mushroom
Hed hunu	Tree ears mushroom
Hed nang lom	Straw mushroom
Hed pa	Wild mushroom
Hed thaan	Truffle
Hoa cham	Lily buds
Houa karod	Carrot
Hua ka lam pii noi	Brussels sprouts
Hua khar	Galanga root (galangal)
Hua navet	Turnip
Hua phark bua	Onion
Hua phark bua deng	Shallot
Hua phark kad	Parsnip
Hua phark kad khao	Beet
Hua phark kat	Rutabaga
Hua phark thiem	Garlic
Khoai mon	Taro root
Mark avacado	Avocado
Mark den	Tomato
Mark euk	Pumpkin
Mark kuai	Eggplant

Mark kuai ngao	Chinese or Asian eggplant
Mark phueak	Yam
Mark pick thai	Pepper
Mark radish	Radish
Mark sa lii	Corn
Mark sa loi	Baby corn
Mark taeng	Cucumbers
Mark thua	Bean
Mark thua yao	Long bean
Mark tua hea	Pea
Marn daang	Sweet potato
Marn fa lank	Potato
Mutar	Mustard
Nai mark thua gnad	Snow pea
Ngod phak	Baby vegetable
Nor mai	Bamboo shoots
Nor mai fa lang	Asparagus
Phark artichoke	Artichoke
Phark brocoli	Broccoli
Phark bua bai	Scallion
Phark bua leuy	Leek
Phark celery	Celery
Phark hom	Spinach
Phark kad ho	Chinese cabbage
Phark ka lam	Kohlrabi
Phark ka lam kuut	Kale

Phark ka lam pii	Cabbage
Phark ka lam dork	Cauliflower
Phark kat khao dork	Flowering Chinese cabbage
Phark kat soom	Fennel
Phark narm	Water spinach or water morning glory
Phark sorrel	Sorrel
Piik thai	Hot pepper
Thua dam	Black bean
Thua khao	White bean
Thua ngor	Bean sprouts
Thua paep	Kidney bean
Thua xang	Mung bean
Thua xang luang	Yellow mung bean

FRUITS

Bai tong	Banana leaves
Mark agnoon	Grape
Mark apricot	Apricot
Mark berry	Berry
Mark berry darm	Blackberry
Mark berry sii fa	Blueberry
Mark cherry	Cherry
Mark chong	Pear
Mark chong fa lung	Quince
Mark chong prickly	Prickly pear

Mark cranberry	Cranberry
Mark date	Date
Mark deuai	Fig
Mark fuang	Star fruit
Mark huung	Papaya
Mark kham	Tamarind
Mark khay	Peach
Mark kien	Grapefruit
Mark kieng	Orange
Mark kieng noi	Kumquat
Mark kieng nuai peui na	Tangerine
Mark kiwi	Kiwifruit
Mark kuai	Banana
Mark marn	Plum
Mark mii	Jackfruit
Mark mo	Melon, watermelon
Mark muang	Mango
Mark nao kiao	Lime
Mark nao leuang	Lemon
Mark nard	Pineapple
Mark nectarine	Nectarine
Mark passion	Passion fruit
Mark phao	Coconut
Mark phueang	Persimmon
Mark piila	Pomegranate
Mark pomme	Apple

Mark raspberry	Raspberry
Mark rhubarb	Rhubarb
Mark strawberry	Strawberry
Mark teang lueang nam pheung	Honeydew
Mark teng	Cantaloupe

GRAINS

Khao ba le	Barley
Khao basmati	Basmati rice
Khao bla	Wheat
Khao buckwheat	Buckwheat
Khao chao	Rice
Khao jao khao	White rice
Khao jao ma li	Jasmine rice
Khao khieab	Hominy
Khao med simon	Brown rice
Khao niao	Sticky or glutinous rice
Khao oat	Oat
Khao oatmju bothanmok	Grits
Khao wild	Wild rice
Paeng sa lee	Cornmeal
Thad peang	Pasta

HERBS AND SPICES

Bai chervil	Chervil
Bai hom sage	Sage

Bai hom savory	Savory
Bai hom thyme	Thyme
Bai juniper	Juniper
Bai khe huud	Lemon basil
Bai laurel	Bay leaf, laurel
Bai lavender	Lavender
Bai marjoram	Marjoram
Bai rosemary	Rosemary
Bai si khai	Lemongrass
Bai tarragon	Tarragon
Dork phark bua bai	Flowering chives
Hua kha	Galanga root (galangal)
Huong liu	Five-spice powder
Ka lii	Curry
Kaen cumin	Cumin
Kaen dork chan	Anise, star anise
Kaen hua bua	Lotus seeds
Kaen mark clove	Clove
Kaen mark mace	Mace
Kaen mustard	Mustard seed
Kaen phark hom poom	Coriander seed
Kaen phik thai	Peppercorn
Kaen phik thai si bua	Pink peppercorn
Kaen poppy	Poppy seed
Kheuang hoam	Allspice

Khi minh	Saffron
Kiing	Ginger
Kiing noi, kiing oan	Lesser ginger
Mark khaeng	Caraway
Mark naeng	Cardamom
Mark phed ngai	Paprika
Mark phet	Chilies
Mark phet porn	Chili powder
Mark phik thai cayenne	Cayenne
Med mark nga	Sesame seed
Obxeui	Cinnamon
Phark bua bai	Chives
Phark bua bai chin	Chinese chives
Phark etuu	Basil
Phark etuu holy	Holy basil
Phark etuu kha, phark bualapha	Thai or Asian basil
Phark hom laap	Tropical mint
Phark hom parsley	Parsley
Phark hom salanea	Mint
Phark si	Dill
Phong turmeric	Turmeric
Puak mark nutmeg	Nutmeg
Rau ngo/mui	Cilantro
Ta kun phark siean	Capers

NUTS

Kaen mark muang hin ma phanh	Cashew
Mark almond	Almond
Mark ko	Chestnut
Mark ko gnai	Walnut
Mark nutt	Nut
Mark pao	Coconut
Mark pecan	Pecan
Mark pistachio	Pistachio
Mark thua dinh	Peanut
Thua dinh bod	Pine nut

MISCELLANEOUS INGREDIENTS

Cheoa kapic	Shrimp paste
Chieo ca ri	Curry paste
Chieo mark phet	Chili paste
Houa phark bua dong	Sweet-and-sour pickled scallions
Hua phark kad horseradish	Horseradish
Kalum pii dong	Pickled Chinese cabbage
Keua	Salt
Khao khoua bodd	Roasted rice powder
Khao kiab koung	Shrimp chips
Kreem mark phao	Coconut cream

Kung haeng	Dried shrimp
Mark karm	Tamarind
Mark olive dam	Black olives
Mark olive kiao	Green olives
Narm chieo thua nuao	*Hoisin* sauce
Narm dork mai	Flower water
Narm kathi mark phao	Coconut milk
Narm manh	Oil
Narm manh canola	Canola oil
Narm manh hoai	Oyster sauce
Narm manh mark nga	Sesame oil
Narm manh mark olive	Olive oil
Narm mark den	Ketchup
Narm mark lene	Hot pepper sauce
Narm mustard	Mustard
Narm pa	Fish sauce
Narm pa dong kem	Anchovy sauce
Narm pa kung	Shrimp sauce
Narm sa iu	Soybean sauce
Narm sa iu dam	Soy sauce
Narm sa iu nieo	Steak sauce
Narm som	Vinegar
Narm som balsamic	Balsamic vinegar

Narm som khao	Rice vinegar
Narm som wine	Wine vinegar
Narm tan kone	Rock sugar
Narm thua leuang	Yellow bean sauce
Narm worcestershire	Worcestershire sauce
Oia	Sugarcane
Phark mo noi	Grass jelly
Phean gio	Rice paper
Sen furr, sen khao poon	Rice noodles
Sen lorn	Cellophane noodles
Sen mii	Egg noodles
Sen mii leuang	Bean thread noodles
Thach hoa	Agar-agar
Thua hu	Tofu

SPECIAL DIETS

Ahanh thi phot sanh kemi	Macrobiotic
Bo kin siin	Vegetarian
Bo mi khai marn	Nonfat
Bo mi thart narm tarn	Sugar free
Calorie tamh	Low-calorie
Khai man tamh	Low-fat
Khao ba lae	Wheat/gluten free
Lok phae	Allergy

Pa sa chark that nom	Dairy free
Phouak bo kin siin sad	Vegan
Phouak keen tae mark mai	Fruitarian
Phouak phae khao ba lae	Wheat allergy
Sodium tamh	Low-sodium
Thart phae	Allergic
Thart siin suung	High fiber

Cambodian Cuisine

CAMBODIAN FOOD MIGHT well be described as one of the most original Southeast Asian cuisines. Whereas Thai food has evolved into complex dishes that create a variety of flavors, Cambodian food tends to rely on simpler ingredients and basic cooking techniques. Cambodian cuisine is also an evolving one, in great part due to the historical influences from India, China, and New World explorers. Also, the terrible military and political ravages of the recent past wiped out many parts of the culture, among them many culinary practices of the upper classes. Traditionally, there were great differences between traditional peasant food in the country and the modern food of the city. The origin of many dishes can be traced to one place or the other. Today in

Cambodia, however, the continuing turmoil is blurring distinctions between the new and the traditional. Therefore, Cambodian restaurants both in America and Cambodia reflect cooking that has adapted to all sorts of new influences.

The staple food of Cambodian cuisine is rice, particularly jasmine rice. Fish—especially freshwater fish—is the primary source of protein. Influences from India gave Cambodia its curries, and the native ingredients of lemongrass, galanga root, kaffir lime, shallots, and garlic are added to produce a uniquely Cambodian taste. China contributed soy sauce, noodles, and cooking techniques such as stir-frying and steaming to supplement the traditional grilling. The explorers of the New World brought chilies, corn, potatoes (especially sweet potatoes), peanuts, and beans. Thailand's influence near the border shows up in some hotter and sweeter foods, and the French colonial presence in Indochina left behind a love of French bread. Like other Southeast Asian cuisines, Cambodian food offers contrasts in flavors and textures that don't often show up in Western food—fresh bean sprouts and greens on noodle soup, fried shallots atop a stir-fry.

The most common seasoning in Cambodia—no surprise here—is *tuk tray* (fish sauce). Other fermented fish products are also very popular. *Prahok*, a fish paste, is quintessentially Cambodian, giving a depth of flavor to all sorts of dishes in the way that anchovies enrich Caesar salad dressing. True to its past, Cambodian cuisine still clings to such old-world favorites as peppercorns and mustard seeds. The most common dipping sauce, *tik marik,* is made from black pepper, salt, and lime juice. Other Southeast Asian countries use mostly chili-based dipping sauces, such as the Vietnamese *nuoc cham.*

Cambodians serve food all at once. Of course, restaurants in the United States will offer courses in the Western style, using many traditional snacks and light items as appetizers. Utensils are a fork, spoon, and chopsticks. The fork is used to push food onto the spoon.

As Cambodian restaurants proliferate in the United States, they will undoubtedly offer more and more dishes that demonstrate the range of the Cambodian chefs.

What Makes It Cambodian: Special Ingredients in Cambodian Cuisine

WHILE THERE AREN'T MANY foods exclusively found in Cambodian cooking, a few that really give the cuisine its distinct flavor follow.

KROEUNG

A spice paste made of lemongrass, galanga root, turmeric, garlic, and shallots. Made fresh in Cambodian kitchens daily, *kroeung* balances different proportions of each spice, depending on the desired flavor of the dish in which it is used.

PRAHOK

Preserved fish, a thick, pasty ingredient that probably most clearly defines the taste of Cambodian food. Alone, it's extremely strong in flavor and odor. But in sauces it lends great depth and body. The best comparison is the effect that anchovy paste has in Caesar salad dressing or in pasta *puttanesca*, a spicy Italian dish.

SUN DIKE DEI

Peanuts. Brought from the New World, peanuts have been assimilated into Cambodian cuisine and are essential to many dishes.

TIK MARIK

A black pepper and lime dipping sauce that, along with *prahok,* probably most distinguishes the flavor of Cambodian cuisine from that of its neighbors.

TIK PRAHOK

A dip made from fermented fish, lime juice, chilies, lemongrass, and cilantro.

TRAY

Fish. The most common types used are mudfish and catfish (*tray unduing, tray sundie*), two of the many favorite fishes in Cambodia. In the United States, farm-raised catfish and tilapia are common substitutes.

TUK TRAY

Fish sauce, much the same as throughout the region.

UNG-KA-A KRA-OP

Jasmine rice; the preferred rice of Cambodia.

Typical Dishes

AAMOK

Curried, steamed fish, generally trout. The curry consists of coconut milk, galanga root, lemongrass, limes, garlic, kaffir lime leaf and peel, *tuk tray,* and chilies. A simpler curry than those usually found across Southeast Asia.

BAI DAM–NERB KHRUP KHNAO

Sticky rice and jackfruit wrapped in banana leaves and grilled. Coconut milk and sugar make this a delightful pudding.

CHAA BAI MREAH PREOO

Egg-and-basil fried rice, seasoned with garlic, chilies, *tuk tray,* and holy basil.

CHAA MEE BHAMPONG

Stir-fried noodles, pork, dried shrimp, squid, beanshoots, and *tofu.*

CHAANG TJOOMNEE TJROOK BHAMPONG

Sweet-and-sour spareribs, similar to a Chinese sweet-and-sour, but the spareribs are deep-fried. Truly sumptuous.

LOC LAC

Stir-fried pork served with raw vegetables.

MEE CHAA

Stir-fried noodles with assorted vegetables, seasoned with garlic, chilies, and soy sauce.

MOAN CHAA KHNYEY

Stir-fried chicken with ginger.

MOAN CHAA KREUNG

Curried chicken with bell peppers and roasted peanuts.

MOAN DOT

Chicken braised with lemongrass and oyster sauce, served with dipping sauces.

NJOAM MA-KAK TRAY ANG

Smoked fish that is deep-fried and mixed with fresh carrots, onions, and green mango, dressed with the usual *tuk tray,* sugar, cilantro, lime juice, and chilies, and served on lettuce leaves. A spicy yet very refreshing salad.

PLEA SAJ KO

Grilled beef sliced very thin and tossed with *tuk tray,* lime juice, sugar, onions, and chilies, served warm on lettuce leaves.

SAJ KO TIK PRAHOK

Intrinsically Cambodian cooking, sizzled beef is placed over a platter of raw vegetables, such as long beans, cabbage, plantains, scallions, eggplant, bean sprouts, and greens. The hot cooked meat with raw vegetables is a wonderful texture experience for the Western palate.

SAMLOR CH-NANG DEIY
A delightful Cambodian stew reminiscent of a French *pot au feu*, with beef, noodles, water spinach, Chinese cabbage, assorted vegetables, holy basil, and cilantro.

SAMLOR PSA-TJAM BUNG
Hot-and-sour straw mushroom and tomato soup with lemongrass, galanga root, and cilantro.

SAMLOR TROPEANG
A curry of small, whole fish, served over rice. The curry is a simple one of coconut milk, tamarind, lime juice, *tuk tray,* and sugar. Vegetables used might include baby corn, bamboo shoots, and scallions.

TRAY PRAMAR TJAMHOY
An open-faced omelette with pork, served with raw vegetables on the side.

TROP BHAMPONG TYEIMOO-OY PONG TEE-E
Fried pancake made with egg-battered eggplant slices.

Glossary

MEATS

Beef—*Saj ko*

Beh dong	Heart
Saj k'baay pleauw	Porterhouse, sirloin
Saj ko kream	Flattened, dried beef
Saj ko tjoom-nut	Steak
Saj kraak saj ko	Beef sausage
Saj kraum poo-oh	Flank steak
Saj pleauw	Chuck (shoulder), round
Saj tjoom loak	Fillet, tenderloin
Thlam'	Liver
Tya-ang tjoom-nee	Rib

Lamb—*Kon tjee-emb*

Kha-a saj tjee-emb	Stew
Khmu-ung tjoeung tjee-emb	Shank
Saj kno-ong tjee-emb	Loin, saddle
Saj smu-u tjee-emb	Shoulder
Saj tjee-emb	Mutton
Saj tjoom nut kno-ong tjee-emb	Loin chop
Saj tjoom nut tju-ung tjoom nee tjee-emb	Rib chop

Tjoom-nut saj tjee-emb	Chop

Pork—*Saj tjhrook*

Cha-ang tjhoomnee tjhrook	Spareribs
Saj bei tjhoan	Bacon
Saj khno-ong tjhrook	Loin
Saj kraak	Sausage
Saj kraak saj tjhrook	Pork sausage (sweet)
Saj pleau tjhrook	Fresh ham
Saj tjhrook tjhaa-ar	Smoked ham
Sbike tjhrook	Pork skin
Tjha-ang tjoom nee tjhrook	Barbecued spareribs
Tjoom-nut saj tjhrook	Chop
Tro-tjeek tjhrook	Ears

Chicken—*Moan*

Cha-ang khno-ong moan	Cutlet
Kreung khnoang moan	Giblets
Kro peh moan	Gizzard

Krun-yaam thjueng moan	Foot
Moan krioo	Capon
Moan n-yee	Hen
Phleau moan	Leg
Saj phleau moan	Thigh
Saj thjoeung moan	Drumstick
Saj troong moan	Boneless breast
Slaap moan	Wings
T-hlam moan	Liver
Troong moan	Breast

Turkey—*Moan barang*

Cha-ang khnoang moan barang	Cutlet
Troong moan barang	Breast

Veal—*Kon ko*

Khmu-ung tjeung kon ko	Shank
Loom-peng kon ko	Kidneys
Phleau kon ko	Leg
Saj cha-ang khnoang kon ko	Cutlet
Saj khnoang kon ko	Loin
Saj kon ko	Breast

Saj smu-u kon ko	Shoulder
Saj tjoom-nut kon ko	Chop
Thlum' kon ko	Liver

Goat—*Po-pe-e*

Saj tjoom-nut po-pe-e	Chop
Saj tyum-loak po-pe-e	Saddle

Poultry—*Sut tzlu-up*

K-ngaan	Goose
K-ngaok	Pheasant
Preap	Squab (pigeon)
Sut krootj	Quail
Tee-e	Duck

Game—*Sut pray*

Krobai	Water buffalo
Krobai pray	Buffalo
Sut svaa	Monkey
Tjhloohsh	Venison
Tjhrook pray	Boar
Toonsai pray	Rabbit

Miscellaneous animals

Kun-kie-p	Frog
Pooh	Snake
Un-diek	Turtle/tortoise

SEAFOOD

Fin Fish—*Tray*

Tray bu-luin	Shark
Tray chlonj	Swordfish
Tray kantraap	Grouper
Tray kroom	Carp
Tray kun tru-up	Perch
Tray mukreilu	Mackerel
Tray reel	Herring
Tray sumot	Tuna
Tray tjhom hoi	Sardine
Tray unduing, tray sundie	Catfish
Tray un-du-ut tch-kai	Sole

Shellfish—*Kroong saa-mot*

Bun ko-ong	Lobster
Kh-daam	Crab
Kroong	Mollusk (freshwater)
Kroong saa-mot	Mollusk (sea), also clam, conch, mussel, scallop

Ktcha-ang	Oyster
Kthjaaew	Snail (freshwater)
Kthjaang saa-mot	Snail (sea)
Kum-pouehh	Shrimp
Njee-oo	Cockle
Pro-on	Crayfish, prawn
Trey yee-hue	Cuttlefish, also octopus and squid
Trey yee-hue kream	Dried squid

DAIRY PRODUCTS

Beu	Butter
Karem kai	Ice cream
Tuk duhko	Milk
Pong moan	Chicken egg
Pong sat	Egg
Pong tier	Duck egg
Pong tier kon	13- to 22-day-old egg (with the duck inside)

VEGETABLES

Da-em kon-tyeik	Plantain
Dumb long barang	Potato
Dumb long tchvee-er	Sweet potato
Kaarot	Carrot
Kaarot saa	Turnip (salsify)

Kon poth	Baby corn
Ko-on speik daop	Brussels sprouts
Ktam saa	Garlic
Ktem	Onion
Leaupeau	Pumpkin, winter squash
Leaupeau veing	Summer squash, zucchini
Mat-te	Pepper
Ma-te hel	Hot pepper
Ma-te plaok	Sweet pepper
Paing puh sraom	Snow pea
Peing pah	Tomato
Pkaa khatnaa	Cauliflower
Pkaa spei	Flowering Chinese cabbage
Poth	Corn
Psatt	Mushroom
Psatt khmu-ew	*Shiitake* or black mushroom
Psatt prey	Wild mushroom
Psatt tjam ba-eung	Straw mushroom
Psatt truttj-eek throok	Tree ear mushroom
Sa-latt	Lettuce
Slaak karot saw	Parsley
Slek ktem	Scallion
Sluk tjroloong	Spinach
Spei	Cabbage
Spei kdaop	Cabbage, savoy
Spei kronj-anj	Kale

Spei saa	Chinese cabbage
Sundaik	Bean, pea
Sundaik bai	Mung bean
Sundaik bundoh	Bean sprouts
Sundaik khmu-ew	Black bean
Sundaik kooa	Long bean
Sundaik saw	White bean
Sundaik seeang	Soy bean
Sundaik seen	Yellow mung bean
Sundaik sing	Kidney bean
Tem kraa-haam	Shallot
Thai thaw	White radish
Tra koon	Water spinach or water morning glory
Tra-sak	Cucumber
Traap veing	Eggplant
Tro peang reu sei	Bamboo shoots
Tuk sundaik	Soy milk

FRUITS

Dong	Coconut
Khnao	Jackfruit
Krotch kwootj	Tangerine
Krotch ma	Lemon, lime
Krotch po sat	Orange
Krotch qwitj	Mandarin orange
Krotch saot	Kaffir lime

Krotch tlaung	Grapefruit
L-maa-ew	Date
Oeu-luk	Watermelon
Pla-ay kom ping riedj	Sapodilla
Pla-ay koo-lain	Litchi
Pla-ay k-tum	Pomegranate
Pla-ay lehaung	Papaya
Pla-ay menoah	Pineapple
Pla-ay min	Longan
Pla-ay mukhot	Mango
Pla-ay peche	Peach
Pla-ay poire	Pear
Pla-ay pomme	Apple
Pla-ay pootree-e	Jujube
Pla-ay saag ma-oeuw	Rambutan
Pla-ay spoeu	Star fruit
Pla-ay tip	Cherimoya
Pla-ay tjeik	Banana
Pla-ay traa peang buy tjoo	Grape
Pla-ay tru bike	Guava
Slak krotch saot	Kaffir lime leaf
Slak tjeik	Banana leaves
Sva-ai	Mango
Thoo ren	Durian

Tjeik nam vaa	Applebanana
Tra sak ba-a long	Melon, honeydew
Tra sak sroeuwv	Cantaloupe
Um pel	Tamarind

GRAINS

Kraab thoonj' tjeet kun	Grits
Noom ko-o	Kasha
Poat tzngao kom bao kan	Hominy
Sroeu saa-llei	Wheat
Sroeu srong-uy	Oat
Ung-ka-a	Rice
Ung-ka-a krahaam	Brown rice
Ung-ka-a kra-op	Jasmine rice
Ung-ka-a saa	White rice
Ung-ka-a trnaab	Sticky or glutinous rice
Ung-ka-a trnaab khmaeu	Wild rice

HERBS AND SPICES

Khnjei	Ginger
Kraap tjhook	Lotus seeds
Kroeung curry	Curry
Kroeung praam mok	Five-spice powder

Ktjcheu a-em	Cinnamon
Le-me-at-t	Turmeric
Lngo-o khmu-ew	Sesame seed (black)
Lngo-o saa	Sesame seed (white)
Mate hel	Chilies
Mate hel maat	Chili powder
Mate plaa-ook	Paprika
Mudainj	Lesser ginger
Murek'	Peppercorn
Murek' saa	Pink peppercorn
Pkaa katjhai	Flowering chives
Potj ku yaha-aoo	Star anise
Slak karot saa	Parsley
Slak katjhai	Chives
Thjee	Basil (holy, lemon, Thai)
Thjee ang kaam	Lemongrass
Thjee ang wo-ong	Mint
Tjee vun sooy	Cilantro

NUTS

Pla-ay dong	Coconut
Sun dike dei	Peanut

MISCELLANEOUS INGREDIENTS

Bai kreep	Roasted rice powder
Bang kie	Dried shrimp
Bun teh sro yoa	Rice paper

Chook	Lotus
Hoisin sauce	*Hoisin* sauce
Kooy-teeoo, noom bainj tjok	Rice noodles
Kreeb bun ko-ong	Shrimp chips
Kroeung tuksing, preing khtjung	Oyster sauce
Ktem tjhroo'	Sweet-and-sour pickled scallions
Kti' dong	Coconut cream
Ku pi'	Shrimp paste
Masaa-ew tjre-e	Agar-agar
Masaw tchaa	Starch
Mate bok	Chili paste
Meey	Egg noodles
Misooah	Cellophane noodles
Peing pah bok	Ketchup
Preyng	Oil
Preyng lngo-o	Sesame oil
Skaa	Sugar
Skaa kraam	Rock sugar
Skaa thnaot	Palm sugar
Skaa um poeuw	Sugarcane
Spei tjhroo'	Pickled Chinese cabbage
Taw hoo	*Tofu*
Tuk dong	Coconut milk
Tuk khme'	Vinegar
Tuk khme' tuk bai	Rice vinegar

Tuk khme' tuk thnaot	Palm vinegar
Tuk saj ko kee-ap	Steak sauce (squeezed from raw beef)
Tuk see ee-ew	Soy sauce
Tuk seen	Yellow bean sauce
Tuk sun daik	Soybean sauce
Tuk taa-eh	Tea
Tuk trey	Fish sauce
Tuk tray kum-poeuh'	Shrimp sauce
Um bal	Salt
Um pel	Tamarind

SPECIAL DIETS

Kaloria tutj	Low-calorie
Khmeen thjeeat	Sugar free
Khmeen thjeeat khlanj	Nonfat
Khmeen thjeeat musaaew	Wheat/gluten free
Musaaew	Wheat allergy
Ne' men tjoomgoeu toah	Allergic
Ne' men phak tuk da ko	Lactose intolerant
Ne' men see saj saat	Lacto-ovo vegetarian

Ne' men see saj sut	Vegetarian
Ne' see tai bun lae phluy tchoeu	Vegan
Ne' see tai bun lae phluy tchoeu neng tuk dah ko	Lacto vegetarian
Play tchoeu	Fruitarian
Thjeeat khlanj tutj	Low-fat
Thjeeat pruy tutj	Low-sodium
Toah	Allergy
U-haa khmin tuk dah ko	Dairy free

Malaysian Cuisine

MALAYSIA'S THREE PRINCIPAL ethnic groups—Malays, Chinese, and Indians—together with the numerous indigenous groups have created a diverse cuisine. While no longer a part of Malaysia, Singapore also celebrates these cultures and cuisines and has enough restaurants to boggle the mind. Through the years various groups have come to Malaysia and brought their own foods with them. The blending of these influences into the cuisine has shaped present-day Malaysian cooking. The Arabs introduced onions, raisins, almonds, and pistachios. People from India brought their famous spices and curries, and people from China brought soy sauce and wok cookery. Many food items from the New World—such as chili peppers and other members of the

Capsicum genus—were introduced to the Malay Archipelago (which includes both Indonesia and Malaysia) by colonial settlers such as the Portuguese, the Dutch, and the English. Indonesia and Malaysia share many dishes and flavors, and over the years they have contributed heavily to the other's cuisine. From all these origins, the cuisines of the Malay Archipelago delight the palate with wondrous concoctions.

A style of cooking that has gained some publicity recently is called *Nonya*, which derives from the Chinese population living by the Strait of Malacca. Chinese men who arrived there over the years married Malay women, and their children married new Chinese arrivals, so now the population is mostly Chinese in origin. The cooking is basically Chinese, but a lot of Malaysian ingredients are used. Some call *Nonya* the comfort food of Malaysia. Pork is a staple meat, and fried noodles are common.

Traditionally, Malays eat with their right hand, using no utensils. Nowadays, however, a fork and knife are most often used. The country is officially Muslim, so many of the customs have come from that tradition. Normally, a meal consists of soup, a meat or fish course, and vegetable accompaniments. Rice is the staple, as it is for Chinese and Indians in the country. Pork isn't used in traditional Malaysian cooking, although Chinese-origin dishes use a great deal of pork. In fact, the large minorities of Chinese and Indians have their own traditions, and their influence on Malaysian food is unmistakable.

What Makes It Malaysian: Special Ingredients in Malaysian Cuisine

ASAM JAWA

Tamarind paste.

ASAM GELUGUR OR ASAM KEPING

Thin slices of dried tamarind, used for the sour taste.

BUAH KERAS

Candlenut; used for thickening curries. One of its traditional uses is for lamp oil, which is how it gets its English name. Similar to the macadamia nut, but less sweet.

DAUN KADOK

Kadok leaves, usually eaten as *ulams* (salads).

DUAN PANDAN

The pandan leaf, used to give a subtle flavor to rice and desserts. Another important use of pandan leaves in Malaysian and *Nonya* cooking is for coloring. The leaves give a light green hue that is often used to contrast with other natural colorings used in Malaysian desserts, such as white from *santan* (coconut milk) and brown from *gula melaka* (coconut sugar or brown sugar).

HAEKOE
Rojak paste made from shrimp, very strongly flavored.

IKAN KERING
Dried fish used to enhance and deepen the flavors of curries.

KIAM CHYE
Fermented cabbage or mustard greens, similar to the Korean *kimchi*, but much milder.

MEI FUN
Very thin rice noodles, common in soups.

PURI ASAM JAWA
Tamarind purée; a convenient form of the essential flavoring of many Malaysian dishes.

ROTI CANAI
A crispy, griddled flat bread, traditionally used as an eating utensil and often served with spicy curries or as a subsitute for rice.

SAMBAL
A fiery-hot relish used to season foods. In Malaysian cooking, a *sambal* is also a spicy curry, generally containing

chilies, ginger, galanga root, shallots, shrimp paste, and coconut milk.

TAUCHEO

Black beans fermented with lots of salt, sort of like the Japanese *miso*.

Typical Dishes

CILI KETMA

Quintessentially Singaporean, crab in the shell is cooked in a fiery-hot, sweet tomato-based sauce.

DAGING LEMBU GORENG CINA

Stir-fried beef and scallions seasoned with fish sauce and ginger.

EGG SAMBAL

Hard-boiled eggs in a spicy *sambal*.

FOO YONG HAI

Open-faced omelette with crabmeat and bamboo shoots. This dish demonstrates a Chinese influence (*egg foo yung*).

GADO GADO

A vegetable salad with spicy peanut sauce, popular not just in Malaysia but also throughout the region.

JOHORE LAKSA

This *laksa* is especially creamy, made with fish and shrimp.

KAI CHOK

Chicken cooked simply and served with a spicy dipping sauce and rice. This is a great dish for resting the palate from the more complex flavors so common in Malaysian cooking.

KERANG TUMIS DENGAN CILI

Mussels cooked in a garlic and chili sauce.

KUEH PISANG

Banana pudding, often served wrapped in a banana leaf.

LAKSA

Various dishes are called *laksas*. They're basically curried noodle dishes with the noodles showing a Chinese influence, the curry showing an Indian influence, and coconut milk added in the Southeast Asian tradition. They vary in spiciness and creaminess, but any *laksa* is a delicious experience.

LAKSA LEMAK

A classic teaming of shrimp with all the expected seasonings—chilies, lemongrass, galanga root, shallots, shrimp paste, sugar, fish sauce, and coconut milk. It's a close relative of the Thai *tom*.

MEE HOON GORENG

Rice vermicelli stir-fried with various vegetables, seasoned with fish sauce, garlic, and a mild yellow curry. This dish may be spicy or mild.

OPOR AYAM

Chicken curried with all the expected spices of Southeast Asia, and lots of coconut milk.

PULUT HITAM

Black sticky-rice pudding, a staple dessert throughout the region. Not as sweet as the familiar Western version, served with a bit of coconut cream.

RENDANG

A curry in the Southeast Asian style, thick with coconut milk sauce and spicy enough to purify your blood. The name comes from Sumatra, and any *rendang* is some version of a curry.

SAMBAL IKAN

A fish curry, made with garlic, shallots, chilies, lemongrass, fish sauce, shrimp paste, and tamarind. Malaysian *sambals* are generally quite similar to Thai curries.

SAMBAL KAEHAND PANJANG

Shrimp and green bean curry made with chilies, shallots, shrimp paste, peanuts, and coconut milk.

SATAY

The *satay* is a staple of Malaysian cooking (as well as Indonesian, of course). It is perhaps the most popular single food item of the culture. A relative of the *shish kebab*, the *satay* is the Malay version of that Middle Eastern mainstay. Skewered chicken, pork, or beef in a spicy marinade is grilled and served with a peanut sauce. A wonderful and versatile dish, *satay* can be enjoyed as a snack or as an entire meal.

SUP TAUHU

Tofu soup with vegetables

Nonya dishes

Nonya cooking may be found in a Malaysian restaurant, but most often only in *Nonya* restaurants. Malaysian restaurants usually eschew pork, which is essential to *Nonya* cuisine. This is home-style Chinese cooking as it has evolved in Malaysia, possessing some real "comfort" foods.

Chap chai	Stir-fried vegetables in the Chinese style.
Char siew	Chinese barbecued pork
Kiam chai boey	A spicy stew of duck and greens
Lobak	Deep-fried pork rolls
Pie tee	Spicy seafood in hat-shaped pastry

Glossary

MEATS

Beef—*Daging lembu*

Daging bahu; daging cuk	Chuck (shoulder)
Daging batang pinang panggang	Chateaubriand
Daging batang pinang porterhouse	Porterhouse
Daging batang pinang yang paling lembut	Tenderloin
Daging kaki	Round
Daging rusuk	Rib
Daging siap ditulangi	Fillet
Daging sirloin (daging antara bahagian batang pinang dan kaki)	Sirloin
Hati	Liver
Jantung	Heart
Stik	Steak
Stik rusuk, stik lambung	Flank steak

Lamb—*Daging anak bebiri; daging bebiri muda*

Cop; daging (rusuk) dipotong kecil	Chop
Cop daging batang pinang dipotong kecil	Loin chop
Cop rusuk	Rib chop
Daging bahagian rusuk ke kaki	Saddle
Daging bahu	Shoulder
Daging batang pinang	Loin
Daging biri-biri; daging bebiri	Mutton
Daging kaki depan	Shank
Rak (tulang rusuk)	Rack
Stew; rendidih	Stew

Pork—*Daging babi*

Bakon; dendeng babi	Bacon
Bibir	Lips
Cop; daging (rusuk) dipotong kecil	Chop
Daging batang pinang	Loin
Ham	Ham
Ham baru	Fresh ham

Ham salai	Smoked ham
Kulit babi	Pork skin
Rusuk babi barbeku; panggang rusuk babi	Barbecued spareribs
Sosej	Sausage
Sosej Cina	Chinese sausage
Sosej Vietnam	Vietnamese sausage
Tulang rusuk babi	Spareribs

Chicken—*Daging ayam*

Ayam betina	Hen
Daging ayam kembiri	Capon
Daging dada	Breast
Daging dada tanpa tulang	Boneless breast
Giblet; hati, jantung, dan hempedal ayam	Giblets
Hati	Liver
Hempedal	Gizzard
Kaki	Leg
Kaki ayam	Drumstick
Kutlet	Cutlet
Paha	Thigh
Sayap	Wings

Turkey—*Daging ayam belanda*

Dada	Breast
Daging ayam belanda kisar	Ground turkey
Kutlet	Cutlet

Veal—*Daging anak lembu*

Anak limpa	Sweetbreads
Cop; daging (rusuk) dipotong kecil	Chop
Dada	Breast
Daging bahu	Shoulder
Daging batang pinang	Loin
Daging kaki depan	Shank
Ginjal; buah pinggang	Kidneys
Hati	Liver
Kaki	Leg
Kutlet	Cutlet

Goat—*Daging kambing*

Cop; daging (rusuk) dipotong kecil	Chop
Daging bahagian rusuk ke kaki	Saddle

Poultry—*Unggas; ayam-itik*

Anak burung merpati; merpati dara	Squab (pigeon)
Angsa	Goose
Ayam hutan	Partridge
Burung kuang bayas	Pheasant
Burung puyuh	Quail
Burung unta	Ostrich
Itik	Duck

Game—*Binatang buruan*

Arnab	Rabbit
Babi jantan	Boar
Daging rusa	Venison
Kerbau	Buffalo

SEAFOOD

Fin fish—*Ikan bersirip*

Belut	Eel
Ikan bass	Bass
Ikan bass berjalur	Striped bass
Ikan bass laut hitam	Black sea bass
Ikan biru	Bluefish
Ikan duri; ikan semilang	Catfish

Ikan flounder; ***ikan sebelah***	Flounder
Ikan grouper	Grouper
Ikan hadok	Haddock
Ikan halibut	Halibut
Ikan hering	Herring
Ikan John Dory	John Dory
Ikan kakap	Monkfish
Ikan kod	Cod
Ikan mahi-mahi	Mahimahi
Ikan merah	Red snapper
Ikan pollock	Pollock
Ikan pompano	Pompano
Ikan putih	Whitefish
Ikan salmon	Salmon
Ikan selar kuning	Orange roughy
Ikan senohong	Holy mackerel
Ikan shad	Shad
Ikan siakap; ikan kerakap; ikan merah	Perch
Ikan sisa nabi	Sole
Ikan skrod	Scrod
Ikan sturgeon	Sturgeon
Ikan tamban; ikan sadin	Sardine
Ikan tenggiri	Mackerel
Ikan tilapia	Tilapia

Ikan todak	Swordfish
Ikan trout	Trout
Ikan tuna, ikan tongkol	Tuna
Ikan turbot	Turbot
Ikan wahoo	Wahoo
Ikan yu; ikan jerung	Shark

Shellfish—*Kerang-kerangan*

Abalone	Abalone
Kapis; kekapis	Scallop
Kerang	Cockle
Ketam	Crab
Kima	Clam
Konc	Conch
Kupan; siput sudu	Mussel
Kurita	Octopus
Sotong; cumi-cumi	Squid
Sotong katak	Cuttlefish
Tiram	Oyster
Udang	Prawn, shrimp
Udang karang	Lobster
Udang kerai	Crayfish

DAIRY PRODUCTS

Aiskrim	Ice cream
Krim	Cream

Krim campur susu	Half-and-half
Krim kental; krim beku	Clotted cream
Krim pekat	Crème fraîche
Krim putar	Whipped cream
Mentega	Butter
Mentega dijernihkan	Clarified butter
Minyak sapi	Ghee
Susu	Milk
Susu baru; susu penuh	Whole milk
Susu mentega	Buttermilk
Susu skim; susu tanpa lemak	Nonfat milk
Tairu	Sour cream
Yogurt	Yogurt
Majerin	Margarine
Telur	Egg

VEGETABLES

Adas; jintan hitam	Fennel
Akar saderi; akar selderi	Celery root (celeriac)
Articok	Artichoke
(Pucuk) asparagus	Asparagus

Avokado; adpokat	Avocado
Bawang	Onion
Bawang merah	Shallot
Bawang putih	Garlic
Bayam	Spinach
Biji sawi; mustard	Mustard
Bit	Beet
Bit Swiss	Swiss chard
Brokoli	Broccoli
Buah tomatio	Tomatillo
Buah tomato	Tomato
Bunga kubis	Cauliflower
Cendawan; kulat	Mushroom
Cendawan jerami	Straw mushroom
Cendawan liar; cendawan hutan	Wild mushroom
Cendawan shiitake	*Shiitake* or black mushroom
Cendawan trufle; kulat trufle	Truffle
Cili manis	Sweet pepper
Daun bawang	Scallion
Daun bawang kucai; lik	Leek
Daun saderi; daun selderi	Celery
Jagung	Corn
Jagung muda	Baby corn

Kacang	Bean
Kacang hijau	Mung bean, yellow mung bean
Kacang hitam	Black bean
Kacang merah	Kidney bean
Kacang panjang	Bean; long
Kacang pi	Pea, snow pea
Kacang pinto	Pinto bean
Kacang putih	White bean
Kai-lan	Kale
Kaktus nopales	Nopales

Kangkung;
   bayam air
	Water spinach or water morning
	   glory

Karot; lobak merah	Carrot
Keladi; ubi kemali	Yam
Kolrabi	Kohlrabi
Kubis	Cabbage
Kubis Brussels	Brussels sprouts
Kubis Cina	Chinese cabbage
Kubis rutabaga	Rutabaga
Kulat telinga	Mushroom; tree ear

Kuntum teratai;
   kuntum seroja;
   kudup teratai;
   kudup seroja
	Lily buds

Labu	Summer squash, zucchini
Labu air	Winter squash
Labu feringgi	Pumpkin

Lada hitam	Pepper, hot pepper
Lengkuas	Galanga root (galangal)
Lobak	Radish
Lobak jepun; lobak daikon	Daikon
Parsnip	Parsnip
Pucuk rebung	Bamboo shoots
Sawi bunga; sawi manis	Flowering Chinese cabbage
Sawi putih	Bok choy
Sayur muda	Baby vegetable
Sorel; sejenis daun herba	Sorrel
Tauge; kecambah	Bean sprouts
Terung	Eggplant
Terung Cina	Chinese or Asian eggplant
Timun; mentimun	Cucumber
Turnip; lobak putih	Turnip
Ubi keladi	Taro root
Ubi keledek; ubi kastela; ubi jalar	Sweet potato
Ubi kentang	Potato
Ubi sengkuang	Jicama

FRUITS

Beri; buah beri	Berry
Beri biru	Blueberry

Beri hitam	Blackberry
Buah anggur	Grape
Buah aprikot	Apricot
Buah asam jawa	Tamarind
Buah belimbing	Star fruit
Buah ceri	Cherry
Buah delima	Pomegranate
Buah epal	Apple
Buah kiwi	Kiwifruit
Buah kuins	Quince
Buah kurma	Date
Buah mangga	Mango
Buah markisah	Passion fruit
Buah nangka; buah cempedak	Jackfruit
Buah nektarin	Nectarine
Buah pear	Pear
Buah pear berduri	Prickly pear
Buah pic	Peach
Buah pisang kaki; buah kesemak	Persimmon
Buah plum	Plum
Buah raspberi	Raspberry
Buah tin; buah ara	Fig
Daun limau purut	Kaffir lime leaf
Daun pisang	Banana leaves

Kantalop; semangka	Cantaloupe
Kelapa; buah kelapa	Coconut
Kranberi	Cranberry
Lemon	Lemon
Limau gedang	Grapefruit
Limau kumkuat	Kumquat
Limau nipis	Lime
Limau purut	Kaffir lime
Limau tangerin	Tangerine
Nanas; nenas	Pineapple
Oren limau manis	Orange
Papaya; buah betik	Papaya
Pisang	Banana
Rubarb	Rhubarb
Strawberi	Strawberry
Tembikai	Melon
Tembikai casaba	Casaba
Tembikai crenshaw	Crenshaw
Tembikai susu	Honeydew
Tembikai; semangka	Watermelon

GRAINS

Barli	Barley
Beras basmati	Basmati rice
Beras ceruh	Brown rice

Beras jasmin	Jasmine rice
Bijian jagung kering	Hominy
Gandum	Wheat
Gandum bulghur; burghul	Bulgur
Gandum kuda bakar	Kasha
Gandum kuda; buckwheat	Buckwheat
Jagung hancur	Grits
Jagung kisar	Cornmeal
Kus-kus	Couscous
Nasi (cooked); *beras* (uncooked grain); *padi* (unmilled grain)	Rice
Nasi beras liar (cooked); *nasi beras hutan* (cooked); *beras liar* (uncooked grain); *beras padi hutan* (uncooked grain)	Wild rice
Nasi putih (cooked); *beras putih* (uncooked grain)	White rice
Oat	Oat

Pasta	Pasta
Polenta	Polenta
Pulut (cooked); *beras pulut* (uncooked grain)	Sticky or glutinous rice
Tepung masa	Masa harina (corn flour)

HERBS AND SPICES

Bijan; lenga	Sesame seed
Biji ketumbar	Coriander seed
Biji sawi	Mustard seed
Biji teratai; biji seroja	Lotus seeds
Buah pala	Nutmeg
Buah pelaga; kepulaga	Cardamom
Bunga kucai	Flowering chives
Bunga lawang	Star anise
Cengkih; bunga cengkih	Clove
Daun kesom	Tropical mint
Daun kesum	Thai or Asian basil
Daun ketumbar	Cilantro
Daun marjoram	Marjoram
Daun pandan	Pandanus
Daun pasli	Parsley
Daun rosemary	Rosemary

Daun salam	Bay leaf
Daun savori	Savory
Daun sej	Sage
Daun serai	Lemongrass
Daun tarragon	Tarragon
Daun thyme	Thyme
Dil	Dill
Epazote; daun teh Mexico	Epazote
Halba	Fenugreek
Halia	Ginger
Jintan	Caraway
Jintan hitam; adas pedas	Fennel
Jintan manis	Anise
Jintan putih	Cumin
Jintan saru	Juniper
Kari	Curry
Kaskas	Poppy seed
Kayu manis	Cinnamon
Kencur	Lesser ginger
Kucai	Chives
Kucai Cina	Chinese chives
Kuntum keper	Capers
Kunyit	Turmeric
Lada; cili; cabai	Chilies
Lada biji	Peppercorn

Lada biji merah	Pink peppercorn
Lada rawit; cayenne	Cayenne
Lengkuas	Galanga root (galangal)
Oregano	Oregano
Paprika	Paprika
Pasli jintan	Chervil
Pokok laurel	Laurel
Pokok lavender; pokok gandaria	Lavender
Pudina	Mint
Rempah allspice	Allspice
Safron; kunyit	Saffron
Selaput biji pala	Mace
Selasih lemon; ruku-ruku	Lemon basil
Selasih; ruku-ruku	Basil, holy basil
Serbuk cili; serbuk lada	Chili powder
Serbuk rempah lima	Five-spice powder

NUTS

Buah badam	Almond
Buah berangan	Chestnut
Buah kelapa	Coconut
Gajus	Cashew
Kacang; kekeras	Nut
Kacang hazel	Hazelnut

Kacang makadamia	Macadamia
Kacang pain	Pine nut
Kacang pekan	Pecan
Kacang pistasio	Pistachio
Kacang tanah	Peanut
Kacang walnut	Walnut

MISCELLANEOUS INGREDIENTS

Acar daun bawang; *jeruk daun bawang* *masam manis*	Sweet-and-sour pickled scallions
Agar-agar	Agar-agar
Agar-agar rumput	Grass jelly
Asam jawa	Tamarind
Belacan; blacan	Shrimp paste
Bihun	Rice noodles
Buah zaitun hijau	Green olives
Buah zaitun hitam	Black olives (ripe)
Budu; pekasam *ikan bilis*	Anchovy sauce
Cuka	Vinegar
Cuka beras	Rice vinegar
Cuka perisa *keembung*	Balsamic vinegar
Cuka wain	Wine vinegar
Esens bunga	Flower water
Garam	Salt

Gula batu	Rock sugar
Kepala santan	Coconut cream
Keropok udang *kropok udang*	Shrimp chips
Kertas tepung	Rice paper
Kicap	Soy sauce
Kubis cina asin; *jeruk kubis cina*	Pickled Chinese cabbage
Lobak pedas	Horseradish
Mi; mi halus	Bean thread noodles
Mi telur	Egg noodles
Minyak bijan	Sesame oil
Minyak kanola	Canola oil
Minyak masak	Oil
Minyak zaitun	Olive oil
Mustard; serbuk *biji sawi*	Mustard
Rempah kari *(basah); pes kari*	Curry paste
Sambal cili; lada *giling; cabai giling*	Chili paste
Santan	Coconut milk
So'un	Cellophane noodles
Sos hoisin	*Hoisin* sauce
Sos ikan	Fish sauce
Sos kacang	Yellow bean sauce

Sos kicap; sos kacang soya	Soybean sauce
Sos stik	Steak sauce
Sos Tabasco	Tabasco® sauce
Sos tiram	Oyster sauce
Sos udang; cencaluk	Shrimp sauce
Sos Worcester	Worcestershire sauce
Tauhu	*Tofu*
Tebu	Sugarcane
Tepung bertih	Roasted rice powder
Tomato sos	Ketchup
Udang kering	Dried shrimp

SPECIAL DIETS

Alah kepada; beralergi	Allergic
Alah kepada makanan dari bahan susu	Lactose intolerant
Alah kepada makanan dari gandum	Wheat allergy
Alahan; alergi	Allergy
Gandum/tanpa gluten	Wheat/gluten free
Kurang lemak	Low-fat

Kurang natrium	Low-sodium
Makrobioti	Macrobiotic
Pemakan hanya buahan	Fruitarian
Pemakan hanya sayuran	Vegetarian
Pemakan hanya sayuran dan buahan	Vegan
Rendah kalori	Low-calorie
Tanpa bahan susu	Dairy free
Tanpa gula	Sugar free
Tanpa lemak	Nonfat
Tinggi kadar serabut; tinggi kadar serat	High fiber
Vegetarian yang memakan juga makanan dari bahan susu	Lacto vegetarian
Vegetarian yang memakan juga makanan dari bahan susu dan telur	Lacto-ovo vegetarian

Indonesian Cuisine

PERHAPS THE SINGLE MOST distinctive aspect of Indonesian cuisine is its diversity. Indonesia's immense size, its huge number of islands, and individual geographies and cultures, along with influences from several ethnic groups through the years, have all helped to create this diversity. Alongside Muslim cooking, with its prohibition against pork, is Hindu-based cuisine, with its love of pork, and so on. Among the groups that have influenced the evolution of Indonesian cuisine are Chinese, who contributed stir-fries and other wok cookery; Indians, with their myriad aromatic spices; Arabs, whose *kebabs* inspired the *satay*; the New World explorers, with their peanuts, chilies, and potatoes; and Dutch, whose love of great feasts helped create the famous *rijstaffel*. The result is one of the spiciest and tastiest cuisines imaginable, with a seemingly endless variety of foods, yet absolutely representative of Southeast Asia.

The staple food of Indonesia is rice. No other Southeast Asian country is more emphatic about its rice—the whiter and fluffier, the better. A typical meal consists of several dishes, many of them fiery-hot, that go with the rice. In this way, the philosophy is much like that of Thais, who also eat large quantities of rice and small amounts of accompaniments. To Americans who find the food too spicy, the best advice is to eat more rice, as the Indonesians do.

As with other Southeast Asian cuisines, fish is a staple protein source. One of the great Indonesian methods of fish cooking is to wrap it in banana leaves with any number of seasonings and grill it. Frying, stir-frying, and steaming are also common. Virtually all the types of fish dishes found throughout Southeast Asia are found in Indonesia, where the melting pot of cultures offers a vast array of foods.

A central cooking philosophy in Indonesian food is to pair up contrasting flavors and textures. Sweet, spicy, and sour flavors and soft or crunchy textures create a wonderful sensation on the palate. Javanese style is sophisticated with complex flavors and sweet-and-sour dishes. Sumatra, with its Indian and Arabian influences, tends to feature hearty fare, with lamb and beef curries, extremely hot and spicy tastes, and a liberal use of cumin, cilantro, and lemongrass. Balinese food uses a great deal of pork, which stems from its Hindu traditions. The famous roast suckling pig is from Bali, where lots of fresh fruits and vegetables are served with the spicy food. Food from Irian Jaya and the Moluccas tends to be on the bland side, with sago flour and cassava root frequently used. These dishes make a nice counterpoint to the spicy foods, so that an Indonesian meal has a very satisfying mix of flavors.

What Makes It Indonesian: Special Ingredients In Indonesian Cuisine

INDONESIANS USE MOST of the same ingredients as the rest of Southeast Asia. Often, dishes resemble those of other countries, but Indonesians emphasize a particular seasoning or spiciness to give their dishes a unique flavor.

ADAS

Fennel leaves, the fresh young ones, along with the flowers.

ASAM

Tamarind, popular for the many dishes requiring a sour accent.

BENGKUANG

A tuber with a slightly sweet taste, quite starchy, used in *rujak*.

CUKA

A clear vinegar widely used to impart the sour taste found in so many dishes.

KECAP

Soy sauce, although the word is the same as the English "ketchup." The word traveled from Malaysia to Europe with sailors, and many vinegar-based sauces were called "ketchup." Tomatoes were added much later to create the modern Western ketchup that we Americans all know and love.

KECAP ASIN

A salty soy sauce.

KECAP MANIS
A sweet sauce made from soy sauce and brown sugar.

KRUPUK
A puffy cracker used as bread. The dough is made from fish flakes and sago flour, rolled thin, then fried so that it puffs up into ladle shapes. A light-tasting and crunchy treat, and great as a scoop for dips.

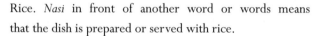

NASI
Rice. *Nasi* in front of another word or words means that the dish is prepared or served with rice.

TAUCO
Salted beans, either black or yellow, essentially the same as the Chinese product. Often used with or instead of soy sauce for a deeper flavor.

TEMPEH
A fermented soy product that is less processed than *tofu*, with whole soybeans in the block. With a rich, nutty flavor, *tempeh* is a great source of protein and is very popular in Indonesian cooking.

TERASI
Shrimp paste, essential to many dishes for the depth of flavor it imparts.

Typical Dishes

AYAM PANGGANG
Grilled chicken in soy sauce.

CAP CAI
Chop suey, a stir-fried dish of Chinese inspiration.

CUMI-CUMI ISI
Stuffed squid.

GORENG CUMI-CUMI
Fried squid that have been marinated in tamarind water seasoned with ginger, chilies, shallots, garlic, and soy sauce. A very tasty treatment for squid.

GULAI UDANG
Shrimp and vegetable curry in coconut milk.

KARI
A curry, almost always very hot.

KARI AYAM
Chicken curry.

KARI KAMBING ACEH
Lamb curry, very hot.

KROKET DAGING

More or less a croquette, a cake made from chopped beef and potatoes and deep-fried, generally served with a peanut sauce.

MARTABAK

A stuffed, grilled turnover of sorts, filled with meat, onions, and eggs. The dough is similar to strudel dough.

MIE GORENG

Noodles fried with coconut milk, meat, tomatoes, cucumbers, and eggs, and seasoned with shrimp paste and chilies.

NASI CAMPUR

A basic dish of steamed rice served with any number of accompaniments, such as meat or seafood, vegetables, fried onions, roasted peanuts, and shredded coconut.

NASI GORENG

Fried rice with meat, tomatoes, cucumbers, and eggs, seasoned with shrimp paste and chilies. One of the most popular dishes among Indonesians, who eat *nasi goreng* or *mie goreng* almost daily.

OTAK OTAK

A fish cake wrapped in a banana leaf and grilled.

PAIS UDANG

Shrimp that are highly seasoned with a paste of galanga root, ginger, chilies, lime, and basil, wrapped in a banana leaf and grilled. The result is an intensely flavored and moist dish.

REMPAH REMPAH UDANG

Fritters made of shrimp and bean sprouts, highly seasoned. Often part of a *rijstaffel*, or served as hors d'oeuvres.

RENDANG

Beef cooked with a lot of spices until it's dry. Buffalo would be used in Indonesia. Beef cooked this way will keep without refrigeration. *Rendang* is served with rice.

RIJSTAFFEL

Literally, "rice table" in Dutch. In Dutch colonial days, enormous buffets of hundreds of dishes were served, with rice as the starting point. Today, 10 to 20 dishes would be the norm. Basically, rice is the main ingredient, and lots of different dishes accompany it, from mild and sweet to hot and spicy.

SAMBAL

The general meaning of *sambal* is a fiery-hot relish used as an accompaniment, but, as in Malaysia, *sambal* can also mean an extremely spicy curry, often with coconut milk, similar to the Thai style.

SAMBAL GORENG UDANG

Spicy shrimp curry with snow peas, green beans, or other Asian vegetables.

SAMBAL KERING TEMPEH

Very spicy dish of fried *tempeh* and potatoes.

SEMUR DAGING

Stir-fried beef with vegetables.

SOTO AYAM KUDUS

Shredded-chicken soup with noodles.

UDANG GORENG

Deep-fried shrimp seasoned lightly with salt, pepper, and coriander seeds.

Glossary

MEATS	
Beef—*Daging sapi*	
Ati	Liver
Bistik; sepotong daging sapi	Steak
Bistik daging panggul	Flank steak
Daging (pilihan) antara rusuk dan pinggang	Porterhouse
Daging bagian belakang yang tebal dan empuk	Fillet
Daging pinggang	Sirloin
Daging pinggang yang lunak	Tenderloin
Daging punggung	Round
Daging rusuk; iga	Rib
Jantung	Heart
Panggang daging punggung	Chateaubriand
Potongan daging antara leher dan bahu	Chuck (shoulder)

Lamb—*Daging anak domba; daging anak biri-biri*

Daging bagian rusuk ke pinggang	Saddle
Daging bahu; daging pundak	Shoulder
Daging biri-biri; daging domba	Mutton
Daging kaki depan	Shank
Daging pinggang	Loin
Daging tulang rusuk	Rack
Potongan daging kecil-kecilan	Chop
Potongan daging tulang rusuk; potongan iga	Rib chop
Potongan kecil daging pinggang	Loin chop
Stuw; styuw; setup	Stew

Pork—*Daging babi*

Bibir	Lips
Daging paha babi (biasanya diasinkan)	Ham
Daging paha babi baru (biasanya diasinkan)	Fresh ham

Daging pinggang	Loin
Ham daging paha babi salai	Smoked ham
Kulit babi	Pork skin
Panggang tulang iga babi	Barbecued spareribs
Potongan daging kecil-kecilan	Chop
Sepek; daging babi yang diasin dan dikukus	Bacon
Sosis	Sausage
Sosis Cina	Chinese sausage
Sosis Vietnam	Vietnamese sausage
Tulang rusuk babi	Spareribs

Chicken—*Daging ayam*

Ati	Liver
Ayam betina; induk ayam; babon	Hen
Dada ayam tanpa tulang	Boneless breast
Daging ayam kebiri	Capon
Daging dada	Breast
Empedal	Gizzard
Jeroan ayam	Giblets
Kaki	Leg

Kaki ayam	Drumstick
Paha	Thigh
Sayap	Wings
Sayatan	Cutlet

Turkey—*Daging kalkun; daging ayam belanda*

Dada	Breast
Daging kalkun giling	Ground turkey
Sayatan	Cutlet

Veal—*Daging anak sapi; daging anak lembu*

Ati	Liver
Dada	Breast
Daging bahu; daging pundak	Shoulder
Daging kaki depan	Shank
Daging kelenjar perut; daging kerongkongan anak sapi	Sweetbreads
Daging pinggang	Loin
Ginjal; buah pinggang	Kidneys
Kaki	Leg
Potongan daging kecil-kecilan	Chop
Sayatan	Cutlet

Goat—*Daging kambing*

Daging bagian **rusuk ke pinggang**	Saddle
Potongan daging **kecil-kecilan**	Chop

Poultry—*Unggas; ayam-itik*

Anak burung **merpati; merpati** **dara**	Squab (pigeon)
Angsa	Goose
Ayam hutan	Partridge
Burung pegar; **ayam pegar;** **burung kuau**	Pheasant
Burung puyuh	Quail
Burung unta	Ostrich
Itik	Duck

Game—*Binatang buruan*

Babi jantan	Boar
Banteng; kerbau	Buffalo
Daging rusa	Venison
Kelinci	Rabbit

SEAFOOD

Fin fish—*Ikan besirip*

Ikan bandeng	Bass
Ikan bandeng bejalur	Striped bass
Ikan bandeng laut hitam	Black sea bass
Ikan biru	Bluefish
Ikan duri	Catfish
Ikan grouper	Grouper
Ikan hadok	Haddock
Ikan haring	Herring
Ikan hiu	Shark
Ikan John Dory	John Dory
Ikan kakap	Monkfish
Ikan kod	Cod
Ikan lemuru; ikan sarden	Sardine
Ikan lidah	Sole
Ikan lindung; ikan mua; belut	Eel
Ikan mackerel	Mackerel
Ikan mahi-mahi	Mahimahi
Ikan merah	Red snapper
Ikan mujair	Tilapia
Ikan orange roughy	Orange roughy
Ikan pecak	Halibut

Ikan pollock	Pollock
Ikan pompano	Pompano
Ikan putih	Whitefish
Ikan salem; ikan salam	Salmon
Ikan sebelah; ikan laut yang gepeng	Flounder
Ikan shad	Shad
Ikan skro	Scrod
Ikan sturgeon	Sturgeon
Ikan todak	Swordfish
Ikan tongkol	Tuna
Ikan trout	Trout
Ikan turbot	Turbot
Ikan wahoo	Wahoo
Sejenis ikan merah	Perch

Shellfish—*Kerang-kerangan*

Cumi-cumi	Squid
Ikan gurita; mangsi	Octopus
Keong besar; siput besar	Conch
Kepiting; ketam	Crab
Remis	Scallop
Remis; kepah	Mussel
Remis besar; kijing	Clam
Sotong mangsi	Cuttlefish

Tiram	Cockle, oyster
Tiram laut	Abalone
Udang	Prawn, shrimp
Udang karang	Crayfish
Udang karang laut	Lobster

DAIRY PRODUCTS

Dadih	Buttermilk
Eskrim	Ice cream
Krem; kepala susu	Cream
Krem beku; kepala susu beku	Clotted cream
Krem campur susu	Half-and-half
Krem pekat	Crème fraîche
Krem putar	Whipped cream
Mentega	Butter
Mentega dijernihkan	Clarified butter
Minyak sapi	Ghee
Susu	Milk
Susu asam	Sour cream
Susu masam (kental)	Yogurt
Susu murni	Whole milk
Susu yang telah diambil kepala susunya	Nonfat milk

Margarina	Margarine
Telur	Egg

VEGETABLES

Adas	Fennel
Advokat; adpokat	Avocado
Akar selederi	Celery root (celeriac)
Asperges; asperjis	Asparagus
Bangkuwang; bangkoewang	Jicama
Bawang; bakung	Onion
Bawang merah	Shallot
Bawang putih; dasun	Garlic
Bayam; bayem	Spinach
Bayam air	Water spinach or water morning glory
Bit	Beet
Blumkol hijau; kobis hijau	Broccoli
Brambang; daun bawang	Scallion
Buah tomat	Tomato
Buah tomatio	Tomatillo
Buncis	Pea, snow pea
Bunga articowk	Artichoke
Bunga sawi Cina	Flowering Chinese cabbage

Cabe manis	Sweet pepper
Cendawan; jamur; kulat	Mushroom
Cendawan jerami	Straw mushroom
Cendawan liar; cendawan hutan	Wild mushroom
Cendawan pohon	Tree ear mushroom
Cendawan shiitake	*Shiitake* or black mushroom
Cendawan trufle; kulat trufle	Truffle
Jagung	Corn
Jagung muda	Baby corn
Kacang	Bean
Kacang hijau; kacang ijo	Mung bean, yellow mung bean
Kacang hitam	Black bean
Kacang merah	Kidney bean
Kacang panjang; kacang polong	Long bean
Kacang pinto	Pinto bean
Kacang putih	White bean
Kaktus nopales	Nopales
Keledek; ubi jalar; ubi manis; rambat	Sweet potato
Kentang	Potato
Ketimun; mentimun	Cucumber
Kocai; bawang perai	Leek

Kol kembang	Cauliflower
Kolrabi	Kohlrabi
Kubis; kol	Cabbage
Kubis Brussel	Brussels sprouts
Kubis Cina	Chinese cabbage
Kubis rutabaga	Rutabaga
Kuncup teratai; kuncup bakung	Lily buds
Labu	Pumpkin
Labu air	Winter squash
Labu ketela; labu gambas	Summer squash, zucchini
Lada hitam; merica	Pepper
Lada pedas; merica pedas	Hot pepper
Laos	Galanga root (galangal)
Lobak cina	Turnip
Lobak jepun; lobak daikon	*Daikon*
Lobak Swis; bit Swis	Swiss chard
Mostar; moster	Mustard
Pucuk rebung	Bamboo shoots
Rades; lobak	Radish
Sawi putih	Bok choy
Sayur muda	Baby vegetable
Sejenis kangkung	Kale
Selederi	Celery

Sorel; sejenis daun herba	Sorrel
Tauge; kecambah	Bean sprouts
Terung	Eggplant
Terung Cina	Chinese or Asian eggplant
Ubi rambat	Yam
(Ubi) talas; keladi	Taro root
Wortel; bortel	Carrot
Wortel putih	Parsnip

FRUITS	
Aberikos; buah aprikot	Apricot
Arbei	Blueberry, strawberry
Asam jawa	Tamarind
Belimbing	Star fruit
Berry	Berry
Berry hitam	Blackberry
Buah anggur	Grape
Buah apel	Apple
Buah ara	Fig
Buah ceri	Cherry
Buah delima	Pomegranate
Buah kesemak	Persimmon
Buah kiwi	Kiwifruit
Buah markisa; markisah	Passion fruit

Buah nangka; buah cempedak	Jackfruit
Buah nectarine; sejenis buah persik	Nectarine
Buah per	Pear
Buah per berduri	Prickly pear
Buah persik	Peach
Buah prem	Plum
Buah quince	Quince
Daun limau purut	Kaffir lime leaf
Daun pisang	Banana leaves
Jeruk besar	Grapefruit
Jeruk kepruk	Tangerine
Jeruk limun	Lemon
Jeruk manis	Orange
Kantelop; semangka	Cantaloupe
Kelapa; buah kelapa	Coconut
Kelembak	Rhubarb
Kurma	Date
Limau	Lime
Limau kumquat	Kumquat
Limau purut	Kaffir lime
Mangga	Mango
Nanas; nenas	Pineapple
Papaya	Papaya
Pisang	Banana
Prambus	Raspberry

Sejenis berry	Cranberry
Semangka	Melon, watermelon
Semangka casaba	Casaba
Semangka crenshaw	Crenshaw
Semangka honeydew	Honeydew

GRAINS

Beras basmati	Basmati rice
Beras pirang; beras merah	Brown rice
Beras yasmin	Jasmine rice
Gandum bulghur	Bulgur
Gerst	Barley
Jagung giling	Cornmeal
Jagung giling kasar	Grits
Jagung untuk bubur	Hominy
Kus-kus	Couscous
Nasi (cooked); *beras* (uncooked grain); *padi* (unmilled grain)	Rice
Nasi beras cerah (cooked); *beras cerah* (uncooked grain)	White rice
Nasi beras liar (cooked); *padi liar* (uncooked grain)	Wild rice

Oat; gandum	Oat
Pasta	Pasta
Polenta	Polenta
Pulut (cooked); *beras pulut* (uncooked grain); *beras ketan* (uncooked grain)	Sticky or glutinous rice
Soba	Buckwheat
Soba bakar	Kasha
Tepung masa	Masa harina (corn flour)
Terigu; gandum	Wheat

HERBS AND SPICES

Adas bintang	Star anise
Adas hitam; adas pedas	Fennel
Adas manis	Anise
Adas putih	Cumin
Bibit teratai; bibit seroja	Lotus seeds
Bijan; wijen	Sesame seed
Biji apiun	Poppy seed
Biji ketumbar	Coriander seed
Biji merica	Peppercorn
Biji mostar; biji moster	Mustard seed

Buah pala	Nutmeg
Bunga lokio; bunga bawang putih	Flowering chives
Bunga pala	Mace
Cabai rawit; lada merah	Cayenne
Cengkeh	Clove
Daun ketumbar; daun seladri; daun selederi	Cilantro
Daun pandan	Pandanus
Daun rosemary	Rosemary
Daun salam	Bay leaf
Daun savori	Savory
Daun sej	Sage
Daun tarragon	Tarragon
Daun thyme	Thyme
Dill	Dill
Epazote; daun teh Mexico	Epazote
Halba	Fenugreek
Jahe; halia	Ginger
Jintan; jemuju	Caraway
Jintan saru	Juniper
Kardamunggu; kepulaga	Cardamom
Kari	Curry

Kayu manis	Cinnamon
Kencur	Lesser ginger
Kuncup kaper	Capers
Kunyit	Saffron
Kunyit; kunir	Turmeric
Lengkuas; laos	Galanga root (galangal)
Lokio; daun bawang putih	Chives
Lokio Cina	Chinese chives
Lombok; cabai; cabe; lada	Chilies
Marjoram	Marjoram
Merica merah	Pink peppercorn
Oregano	Oregano
Paprika; lombok	Paprika
Permen	Mint
Permen tropis	Tropical mint
Peterseli; daun sup	Parsley
Peterseli berbau jintan	Chervil
Pohon lavender; pohon gandaria	Lavender
Pohon salam	Laurel
Rempah berbau campuran (tumbuh di amerika tengah)	Allspice
Selasih limun	Lemon basil

Selasih Thai	Thai or Asian basil
Selasih; ruku-ruku; kemangi	Basil, Holy basil
Serai; sereh	Lemongrass
Serbuk bumbu lima jenis	Five-spice powder
Serbuk cabai; serbuk cabe; serbuk cili	Chili powder

NUTS

Amandel; buah badam	Almond
Biji jambu monyet; kacang mende	Cashew
Buah kelapa	Coconut
Buah kemiri	Hazelnut
Buah kenari	Walnut
Buah kenari hijau	Pistachio
Kacang	Nut
Kacang cemara	Pine nut
Kacang pekan	Pecan
Kacang tanah	Peanut
Kastanye; berangan	Chestnut
Makadamia	Macadamia

MISCELLANEOUS INGREDIENTS

Acar brambang masam manis; asinan brambang masam manis	Sweet-and-sour pickled scallions
Agar-agar	Agar-agar
Agar-agar rumput	Grass jelly
Asam jawa	Tamarind
Bakmi	Rice noodles
Bakmi telur	Egg noodles
Buah zaitun hijau	Green olives
Buah zaitun hitam	Black olives (ripe)
Bumbu kari	Curry paste
Cuka	Vinegar
Cuka anggur	Wine vinegar
Cuka balsem	Balsamic vinegar
Cuka beras	Rice vinegar
Esens bunga	Flower water
Garam	Salt
Gula batu	Rock sugar
Kecap	Soy sauce
Kepala santan	Coconut cream
Kertas tepung	Rice paper
Kerupuk udang; krupuk udang	Shrimp chips
Kubis Cina asin; kubis Cina masin	Pickled Chinese cabbage

Lobak pedas	Horseradish
Mi; mi halus	Bean thread noodles
Minyak bijan	Sesame oil
Minyak kanola	Canola oil
Minyak masak	Oil
Minyak zaitun	Olive oil
Mostar; moster	Mustard
Petis ikan	Anchovy sauce
Sambal chili; sambal oelek; lombok giling	Chili paste
Santan	Coconut milk
Saus bistik	Steak sauce
Saus hoisin	*Hoisin* sauce
Saus ikan	Fish sauce
Saus kacang	Yellow bean sauce
Saus kecap; saus kacang soya	Soybean sauce
Saus Tabasco	Tabasco® sauce
Saus tiram	Oyster sauce
Saus tomat	Ketchup
Saus udang; cencaluk	Shrimp sauce
Saus Worcestershire	Worcestershire sauce
Sohun	Cellophane noodles
Tauhu	*Tofu*
Tebu	Sugarcane

Tepung bertih	Roasted rice powder
Terasi	Shrimp paste
Udang kering	Dried shrimp

SPECIAL DIETS

Alergi; kepekaan	Allergy
Alergis; alergik; peka sekali	Allergic
Gandum / tanpa zat perekat	Wheat/gluten free
Ketidaktoleranan kepada makanan dari bahan susu; peka sekali kepada makanan dari bahan susu	Lactose intolerant
Ketidaktoleranan kepada makanan dari gandum; peka sekali kepada makanan dari	Wheat allergy
Makrobiotik	Macrobiotic

Pemakan hanya buah-buahan	Fruitarian
Pemakan hanya sayur-sayuran	Vegetarian
Pemakan hanya sayur-sayuran dan buah-buahan	Vegan
Pemakan hanya sayur-sayuran yang memakan juga makanan dari bahan susu	Lacto vegetarian
Pemakan hanya sayur-sayuran yang memakan juga makanan dari bahan susu dan telur	Lacto-ovo vegetarian
Rendah kalori	Low-calorie
Rendah lemak	Low-fat
Rendah sodium	Low-sodium
Tanpa bahan susu	Dairy free
Tanpa gula	Sugar free
Tanpa lemak	Nonfat
Tinggi kadar serabut; tinggi kadar serat	High-fiber

Thai Cuisine

THAI CUISINE CAN BE SUMMED UP in very few words: lots of flavor, lots of spice, and lots of rice. Thai chefs combine flavors with great zeal and with the intent of tantalizing the taste buds. A good part of the flavor in Thai food comes from a large variety of fresh herbs. In fact, as the cuisine has evolved during the last seven centuries, the cooks have utilized more and more herbs and spices, and their embracing of new ingredients has created a cuisine that continues to evolve today.

One of the basic principles of Thai cooking comes from the ancient Chinese philosophy of balancing five basic tastes: salty, sour, bitter, spicy-hot, and sweet. This system probably derives from the Indian *ayurveda,* which adds the spicy-hot taste to the four tastes commonly recognized in the West. Thai cooks do balance these tastes, but it's the spicy-hot taste, primarily from chilies, and sourness, from various sources, that really form the basis of the unique flavors we call "Thai."

One aspect of Thai cooking that is not common in the United States is the royal cuisine, which isn't well-known outside Thailand. While actual dishes may not comprise any special ingredients or tastes, the presentations are amazing, with beautifully carved and presented foods. Fruits, especially, are presented in such a beautiful way that they're actually art as well as food.

NOTE Chopsticks are not used in Thailand except when eating Chinese-type noodles. Only a fork and spoon are used, as food is already cut into bite-size morsels, eliminating the need for a knife. The fork is used to move food around the plate, and the spoon to put the food into the mouth. In northern Thailand, people often eat with their hands: Sticky rice is rolled into a ball and used to pick up food and sauces. Until the 19th century, the entire country ate with their hands, using ordinary rice as well as sticky.

What Makes It Thai: Special Ingredients In Thai Cuisine

THERE ARE SEVERAL INGREDIENTS that distinguish Thai cooking. Familiarity with them helps in understanding the cuisine and its special flavors. Some are common in Western cuisine while others have emerged only in the past few years as Southeast Asian food has grown more and more popular.

PRIK AND PRIK THAI

Chili peppers and peppercorn, respectively. Spiciness (as in **hot**) is one of the hallmarks of Thai food. When Thais migrated seven centuries ago from the Yunnan province in southern China to present-day Thailand, they were already familiar with the *prik thai*, the peppercorn, and they found it there as well. After traders brought chilies from the New

World, Thai cooks put them to extensive use. In fact, Thai food has been getting hotter and hotter through the years.

Several varieties of chili peppers, both fresh and dried, are used in different combinations and in pastes and bottled sauces. Peppercorns are still widely used as well, in all their forms, white pepper being the most popular.

? TIP! . . . HELP, MY MOUTH IS ON FIRE!

If you eat chilies and feel that you're on fire, eat something fatty or oily. Buttered bread is good in a pinch, coconut milk may help, or try whole milk. Fried potato or corn chips are good as well. When the burning finally subsides, remember the pain for the next time you feel brave!

If you get peppers on your skin and it's burning, rub with cooking oil, then wash thoroughly. Avoid any contact with your eyes. Keep chilies away from children; they can cause severe burning and skin damage.

Most Thai restaurants use a system to let you know the degree of hotness of menu items. Of course, even "mild" may seem firecracker-hot to the uninitiated.

BAI GKA-PRAO
Holy basil, used in stir-fried dishes; the tiny leaves have a distinct peppery quality with basil overtones.

BAI HORAPA
Thai sweet basil; similar to the Western anise or licorice basil, sort of a blend of basil and anise flavors.

BAI MAENG-LAK

Lemon basil, a light, delicate basil, whose seeds are also used. The seeds are soaked in water and used in soups, adding a tapioca-like consistency.

BAI TOEY

Pandanus leaf. The essence of this leaf can be found in many Thai sweets, much as vanilla is used in Western desserts.

BAI MA-GKROOD AND PEW MA-GKROOD

Kaffir lime leaf and kaffir lime zest. With their distinctive citrus flavors, these ingredients blend very well with lemongrass in many dishes. It's a worthwhile experiment to buy some *bai ma-gkrood* and taste them alongside lemongrass, as well as together. Then you can appreciate the unique flavors and how they enhance Thai food.

CHINESE MUSTARD PICKLE

Vegetables such as cauliflower, carrots, shallots, and green beans pickled in vinegar, garlic, and mustard seeds.

DRIED FISH BELLY

Used in soup, it's very strong-smelling when dry, but once it's in soup it mellows. Likewise, dried shrimp and dried jellyfish are common ingredients.

DTA-KRAI, KAH, BAI MA-GKROOD

Lemongrass, galanga root, and kaffir lime leaves. Although garlic and shallots are the most common herbs in Thai cooking, these are the three that give much of Thai cooking its wonderful, unique flavors. *Dta-krai, kah,* and *bai ma-gkrood* form the base of many curry pastes, and you'll recognize the taste from *dtom yam* (hot and sour shrimp soup) as well as many other soups and salads.

DTA-KRAI

Lemongrass. A long grasslike stalk, imparting, as its name suggests, a delicate, lemony taste. When sliced very thin, it's chewable and used in salads. Many medicinal properties have been ascribed to lemongrass. It's reputed to be an effective treatment for stomach problems, colds, and diabetes.

DTAO JIAO

Yellow bean sauce. Derived from Chinese cuisine, this fermented soybean mixture subtly enhances dishes with saltiness and the robustness of soybeans.

GAPI

Shrimp paste. Very strong in odor, made of fermented shrimp in salt, a little goes a long way. It is used in curry pastes and chili pastes in small quantities to enhance the aroma of the dish being made. *Gapi* makes *nam pla* seem like mild herbal tea.

GRA-THIAM, HOM

Garlic and shallots; the two most oft-used herbs in Thai cooking. *Gra-thiam* and *hom* impart their characteristic depth of flavor on many Thai dishes.

KA-MIN

Turmeric. Used fresh, this root imparts a pungent, earthy taste as well as intense yellow color.

KAH

Galanga root; also called Thai ginger or galangal. It is a close relative of ginger, but more pungent and fiery. Like ginger, it is used to treat cold symptoms and is used as a blood purifier.

KHAO

Rice; the single most important food in Thai cuisine. Thais most often use jasmine rice, an especially flavorful one. As the principal staple food of Asia, it is elevated to an almost spiritual level. Rice is always the central element of the meal, with the other dishes serving as accompaniments or condiments. Although Westerners will eat large amounts of other dishes and small amounts of rice, Thais do just the opposite.

KHAO NIO

Sticky rice, also known as glutinous or sweet rice among other Asians. *Khao nio* is common in northern and north-eastern areas of Thailand, where it is eaten with the hands. Condiments and sauces are then sopped up with the little ball that is rolled between the fingers and palm. In other parts of Thailand, sticky rice is often sweetened for snacks or dessert. Sticky rice is very delicate and fragile. To preserve the individual grains, the rice is soaked in water, then dry-steamed until just tender.

KHAO NIO DAM

A nutty whole grain also known as Indonesian black rice. In Thai cooking it's most often used in black rice pudding.

MA-KAM

Tamarind. Sour varieties of this tropical fruit provide much of the sour in Thai dishes, together with limes. The juice also acts as a tenderizer. Sweet varieties are eaten as a delightful fruit.

MA-MUANG

Mangoes; one of the favorite fruits of Thailand.

NAM MAN HOI

Thai oyster sauce, used as a flavoring in stir-fried vegetables and in meat and seafood dishes. *Nam man hoi* has more oyster flavor and less salt than common Chinese varieties.

NAM PLA

Fish sauce. Without fish sauce, there is no Thai cooking! *Nam pla* is to Thai cooking what soy sauce is to Chinese cooking. It is made by fermenting anchovies with salt and water. As pleasant as it is when used to enhance Thai dishes, it is just as *un*pleasant when spilled and not cleaned up! The stuff really stinks when left sitting around, so keep it capped and stored upright. If you have an aversion to fish sauce, soy sauce can be used as a substitute.

NAM PRIK PAO

A roasted chili paste that adds salty, sweet, and hot flavors to many dishes and can be used as a condiment or spread. It is made from roasted red chilies, dried shrimp, *gapi,* garlic, shallots, tamarind, *nam pla,* and sugar.

NOODLES

Thai cuisine, like other Southeast Asian cuisines, uses a lot of noodles. Noodles can be classified by what they're made with: wheat, rice, or mung bean flour. Wheat noodles can be with or without eggs and resemble western noodles of different shapes. Rice noodles are generally vermicelli, which are very thin sticks, or narrow, flat noodles, known as *chantaboon.* Rice noodles are clear and delicately flavored. Mung bean flour, which is high in protein and low in carbohydrates, is used to make cellophane or glass noodles, which are much like rice noodles but hold up very well even when cooked extensively. They're considered especially good for diabetics because they don't rapidly elevate the blood sugar.

PAK CHEE

Cilantro. Roots, seeds, leaves, and stems are all used in various dishes, especially in many soups and most salads. The roots are used in curry pastes and soup stocks. Also known as coriander or Chinese parsley, *pak chee* has a distinct, light taste and persistent aroma that really stays with you.

PAK BOONG

Water spinach or water morning glory, known as *ong choi* in Chinese. It has a taste that is milder than spinach and a texture similar to watercress. It looks like small, flat spinach leaves.

RICE PAPERS

Used for both fresh and fried spring rolls, these super-thin rice "crepes" are the usual Thai wrapper. Chinese-style egg roll and spring roll skins, which are thicker, may also be used.

SEE IU

Soy sauce. Although fish sauce has become the main source of salt, soy sauces are still commonly used. Before modern transportation, inland areas relied on *see iu* rather than *nam pla*, and it is still a popular source of salt in many of these areas.

THAI EGGPLANT

The eggplant known as Thai eggplant is green and white and about 1½ inches in diameter. The pea eggplant is even smaller, about the size of a cherry tomato, and is often eaten raw. Other types of eggplants of various sizes are used in Thai cooking as well.

THOO-RIAN

Durian; an odd fruit, loved by some and hated by others. It has a thick, hard, brownish green peel. The flesh is custardy, and the odor is rather strong. Your first taste should be of a fresh fruit, not frozen, and chosen by someone who knows when the fruit is at its best.

Appetizers

IN WESTERN CUISINE, the meal starts with appetizers and moves in a linear fashion through dessert. Not so in Thai cuisine. The central focus of the meal is a big bowl of rice, and dishes are chosen that complement or contrast one another. Dishes are served either all at the same time, or as they are prepared.

Thai restaurants in America have adapted somewhat to the Western style of eating. They choose dishes that seem especially appropriate to eat as appetizers and make smaller portions of them. Also, many of the dishes that we list as appetizers are commonly eaten as snacks in Thailand, often from street vendors. Just remember, the placement of dishes as appetizer or main course is arbitrary, so feel free to have your meal served in the traditional Thai style.

GOONG CHEUP PANG TOD
Shrimp dipped in batter and fried, served with sweet-and-sour sauce.

GOONG HAU
Shrimp wrapped in rice paper and fried.

HED YAUNG
Grilled marinated mushrooms with peanut sauce.

HOI MALANG POO SONG KRUONG
Mussels mixed with onion, bell peppers, and cilantro in a very spicy chili-lime sauce.

HOI PRIG PAO
Clams sautéed in spicy garlic-shrimp paste with Thai sweet basil and chili peppers. Three-alarm spice in this one!

KANOM BUENG YUAN
Crispy omelettes made with a batter of coconut milk, rice flour, and eggs. The filling can be any of several ingredients, including coconut, seafood, peanuts, *tofu,* or vegetables.

KHAO GRIAB PAAK MAW

Rice skin dumplings filled with pork, peanuts, garlic, and cilantro, seasoned with fish sauce. The skins are steamed, filled, and eaten in a lettuce leaf. This is a popular dish in the street markets of Bangkok.

MOO PING

Skewered pork, marinated with coconut milk and spices, grilled, served with a spicy-sour sauce.

PLA MUK YAUNG

Squid steak marinated in seasoned coconut milk and grilled. The normal garnish is crushed peanuts and cilantro, served with a spicy chili sauce.

POH PIA SOD

Fresh spring rolls, almost like a salad wrapped up in a thin rice pancake. Ingredients vary but often include any combination of bean sprouts, scallions, *tofu,* carrots, cilantro, basil, cellophane noodles, and cucumbers. Also, pork, chicken, sausage, and shrimp or scallops are often included. Served with sweet and hot sauces.

POH PIA TOD

Crispy, fried spring rolls including various Asian vegetables, noodles, and meat or seafood. The ingredients are stir-fried, and the rolls are wrapped and deep-fried. Served with dipping sauces.

POO NIM

Batter-fried clams with sweet-and-sour garlic-chili sauce.

SAI OAOA

Pork sausage served with lettuce, onions, ginger, lime, peanuts, and chili peppers.

SATAY (SATE)

Grilled, skewered meat. The peanut sauce of the Thai version is spicy, and the skewer is served with cucumber relish.

TAU-HOO TOD

Fried *tofu* with sweet-and-sour chili sauce, garnished with ground peanuts and cilantro.

TOD MUN PLA

Fish cakes made with curry paste, kaffir lime leaf, and green beans, served with fresh cucumber salad.

YUM NUEA NAMTOK

Spicy grilled beef with onions, cilantro, and roasted grains in a spicy and sour sauce.

Soups

GAENG JUED KAI
Pork and egg soup. The eggs are cooked into a flat omelette, then cut into strips.

GAENG JUED PAKKAAD DONG
Chinese mustard-pickle soup, a simple soup made with pork and flavored with fish sauce and garlic.

GAENG JUED TAOHOO
Soup with *tofu,* scallions, and pork.

GAENG JUED WOON SEN
Cellophane noodle soup made with minced pork, enhanced with fish sauce, cabbage, scallions, and cilantro. A very wholesome and refreshing soup, as cellophane noodles seem so light.

GAENG LIANG
A traditional soup of shrimp, shallots, spinach, and basil.

GAENG SOM PLA CHON
Fish soup with tamarind, which imparts a sweet-and-sour taste, served with water spinach.

GEAO NAM MOO

Thai *wonton* soup, the *wontons* filled with minced pork, *bok choy,* bean sprouts, scallions, and cilantro.

KANG JUED PAK

A delicate vegetable soup with pork.

KAPAW PLA

Dried fish belly soup with chicken and bamboo shoots, garnished with sliced eggs and cilantro.

KHAO TOM GOONG

Rice soup with shrimp, flavored with fish sauce, garlic, and cilantro.

KHAO TOM MOO

Rice soup with pork.

KHAO TOM PLA GAPONG

Rice soup with red snapper. A nice light soup that won't weigh you down.

POH TAEK

A soup of mixed seafood, especially shellfish, with a pronounced aroma of lemongrass, galanga root, and kaffir lime leaves.

TOM KHA GAI

Coconut broth with chicken, galanga root, mushrooms, and roasted peppers.

TOM YUM KUNG

This famous hot-and-sour shrimp soup is a Thai institution. There are other *tom yum* soups besides *kung* (shrimp), and all are fiery-hot with flavors of cilantro, kaffir lime, lemongrass, and galanga root. But the broth is light-bodied and refreshing, despite the chilies floating around in it! It really is Thai comfort food.

TOM YUM PLA GROB

Crispy fish spicy soup with lemongrass, galanga root, tamarind juice, and chilies. The fish is bought at market already prepared or prepared by simply deep-frying it. Everything is simmered together.

Noodle and Rice Dishes

THERE ARE MANY and varied noodle dishes in Thai cooking. The best known is *pad thai* (stir-fried rice noodles), but soup noodles are eaten more in Thailand. Most noodle dishes are popular in street markets, and they are eaten throughout the day as a snack. In Thai restaurants in the United States, the noodle dishes are eaten either as appetizers or as part of the main course. Their starchiness makes a nice foil to spicy curries or stir-fries.

Likewise, rice dishes can balance a meal nicely. The

standard rice dish, of course, is plain rice, generally jasmine rice, which is delicious on its own. But there are several tasty rice concoctions eaten as snacks, lunch, or dinner.

KHAO CLOOK GAPI

Fried rice flavored with *gapi,* or shrimp paste, which has quite a strong taste. The dish is then garnished with mango, fried shrimp, sautéed garlic and shallots, strips of thin omelette, and lime. Other garnishes may be used as well. The garnishes go very well with the taste of the rice, and this dish is quite delicious and not overly fishy-tasting.

KHAO MUN GAI

Steamed rice with chicken. The chicken is served atop rice steamed in chicken broth, garnished with scallions and cilantro, and served with fish sauce mixed with chilies and lime juice. Garlic-ginger soy sauce may also be used.

KHAO PHAD GAI LEB KUNG

Chicken-and-shrimp fried rice, very much like Chinese fried rice, but seasoned with fish sauce and garnished with tomatoes, cucumbers, cilantro, and lime. The overall taste comes across as somehow brighter than a Chinese fried rice, perhaps because of the lime and cilantro.

KHAO PHAD PUU

Egg-and-crabmeat fried rice. Another Thai version of fried rice, this time with crabmeat.

MEE GA-THI

Rice noodles with a sauce of shrimp, pork, coconut milk, *tao jeao* (bean sauce), *tofu,* sprouts, shallots, and fish sauce, garnished with chives.

MEE GROB

Fried rice vermicelli mixed with a light sweet-and-sour sauce, put into a bowl, and garnished with strips of omelette, scallions, bell peppers, chives, *tofu,* and cilantro. A very light and refreshing dish.

PAD THAI

Certainly the best-known Thai noodle dish, it is a simple dish made with the basic stir-fry ingredients of garlic, dried shrimp, fish sauce, sugar, tamarind juice, *tofu,* peanuts, bean sprouts, and chives. The cooked noodles are added last and tossed with the other ingredients, then the entire dish is garnished with bean sprouts, lime wedges, chives, and other ingredients according to the cook. A very common dish in Thailand from street vendors, its delightful, refreshing simplicity has made it a favorite among Americans.

PHAN WOON SEN

Stir-fried cellophane noodles, with any sort of ingredient according to the cook, such as meat, seafood, or vegetables, seasoned very simply with fish sauce, and garnished with cilantro. A good balance to spicier dishes.

Thai Yum (Spicy Salads) and Salads

THAI YUM ARE A BIT DIFFICULT to define within the Western definition of salads. A vast array of ingredients is used to shape hundreds of cold or warm dishes that don't fit a category other than "salad." *Thai yum* are spicy, using the fiery-hot bird chilies, but are often toned down a bit for American tastes. *Thai yum* provide wonderful balance in a Thai meal.

LAAB

Diced beef with scallions, chilies, mint, and lime dressing. May include chicken, pork, or beef. A version from the north uses raw buffalo meat.

PLA KUNG

Lemongrass and shrimp salad, with lime juice, fish sauce (surprise!), cilantro, mint, shallots, scallions, and chilies (surprise again!). This salad is delightfully light and refreshing.

SOM TAM

Green papaya salad made by pounding garlic, chilies, dried shrimp, peanuts, and green beans together in a mortar. A sauce of fish sauce, lime juice, and palm sugar is mixed with tomatoes, papaya, and carrots, and that is mixed with the pounded ingredients. This dish is fiery-hot.

YUM DOCK GULAB
Rose petal salad, with chicken, shrimp, pork, chilies, fish sauce, lime juice, peanuts, and cilantro, all served over lettuce leaves

YUM HET HU NUU
Elephant ear salad. A mixture of elephant ear mushrooms, ground pork, shrimp, chilies, shallots, bean sprouts, lime juice, fish sauce, scallions, and cilantro, served over lettuce.

YUM MAKUA YAAW YANG
Grilled eggplants covered with grilled garlic and shallots, and chopped dried shrimp. The dressing is hot and sour, and cilantro is the garnish.

YUM PLA DOOK FOO
Crispy fish salad. The fish is first cooked and flaked, then deep-fried till crispy. The salad is dressed in a typical hot-and-sour sauce.

YUM PLA MUK
Squid salad with lemongrass, shallots, mint, and lime.

YUM PLA TOO
Spicy tuna salad with hot-and-sour flavors predominating. Cooked tuna is tossed with scallions, cilantro, and shallots with a dressing of fish sauce, lime, and chilies.

YUM PRIK YOUACK

Nice and hot, loaded with chilies to purify your blood. Grilled banana peppers, shallots, shrimp, and pork, with coconut cream, fish sauce, and lime juice.

YUM SOM OH

Grapefruit, toasted coconut, cashews, dried shrimp, cooked shrimp, shallots, scallions, chilies, and cilantro. Dressed with fish sauce and lime juice.

Thai Curry

FORGET ABOUT the iridescent yellow-green stew that you called curry in your past life. Thai curries come in all colors and flavors, are (what else?) very hot, and display a wonderful sensuous personality that comes from the rich coconut milk that most (but not all) Thai curries employ. Coconut milk, and especially the cream that comes to the top, adds an incredible richness in the mouth that is best balanced with lighter foods at the same meal. Essentially, curries are hearty, souplike dishes that are eaten with copious quantities of rice. They're made from curry pastes that are created by mashing together various herbs, spices, and other ingredients. Vegetables, meats, and seafoods are stir-fried and mixed with coconut milk (or oil) and the curry paste and *voilà!*—a Thai curry.

Although there are dozens of Thai curries, five are the

most common: *gaeng kiao wahn* (green), *gaeng dang* (red), *gaeng garee* (yellow), *gaeng massaman* (massaman), and *gaeng panang* (panang).

Green curry is perhaps the most typical of Thailand because of its herbal qualities and its extreme heat, along with its thinner, lighter body. While it may burn your mouth, it also feels very light and refreshing. Green curry is especially appropriate for seafood and pork.

Red curry is also very hot and light-bodied, but it is seen most often with poultry.

Yellow curry is the Thai version of "Indian" curry, often including potatoes, and generally used with chicken or beef. The heat can also be intense in yellow curry.

Massaman and *panang* curries trace their origins to the Muslim south. They are usually made with beef or lamb, and they are very thick and rich. These two most resemble Indian curries in their sweet, thick, and aromatic sauces, and they tend to be the least hot.

If you go to Thailand, be sure to sample all the curries you can, especially those not common in America. Two common curries, very hot and not coconut milk-based, are *gaeng som* (sour curry) and *gaeng bpah* (jungle curry). They are both light-bodied with great pungency.

GAENG GAI

Chicken in red curry, which will include chili peppers and Thai basil, along with any of a variety of vegetables.

GAENG GAI BAMA

Burmese chicken curry with red and yellow curry pastes. Especially rich and creamy, not fiery-hot.

GAENG KAREE GAI

Chicken in yellow curry with potatoes and cilantro, along with other vegetables.

GAENG KIAO WAHN LOOGCHIN BPLAH

Green curry with fish dumplings.

GAENG KIAO WAHN MOO

Green curry with pork. Includes Thai sweet basil, kaffir lime leaves, and eggplants.

GAENG MASSAMAN PAE

Massaman curry with goat.

GOUY TEAO GAENG

Chicken and *tofu* in a rich yellow curry, with egg noodles.

PAD PED BPLAH DOOG TOD GRAWP

Fried catfish with red curry sauce.

PANANG NEUR

Panang curry of beef, including Thai basil, kaffir lime leaves, and various vegetables such as baby corn, mushrooms, and tropical fruits.

PANANG PED
Duck in *panang* curry, with kaffir lime leaves and such things as baby corn, straw mushrooms, tomatoes, and pineapple.

Fish and Shellfish Dishes

GAAM POO OB WON SEN
Crab claws baked *en casserole* with garlic, fish sauce, sugar, cellophane noodles, scallions, and cilantro. Simply delicious.

GOONG HOI PAD MAKHAM SOD
Scallops and shrimp in a spicy tamarind-shallot sauce, accompanied by cashews and Asian vegetables.

GOONG PAO NAM PLA WAN
Broiled lobster with a sauce of tamarind, sugar, and fish sauce.

HAW MOK
Fish steamed in banana leaves with a red curry paste and coconut milk sauce. Very rich and creamy with great spice balance.

HOI MALANG POO PAD GRAW PRAW
Nice and spicy mussels with garlic, chilies, and Thai sweet basil.

HOI PAD HED
Stir-fried scallops and assorted vegetables, with varying hotness.

HOI PAD MAKHAM SOD
Scallops, baby corn, and cashews in a tamarind-shallot sauce.

HOI PAD NAM PRIK PAO
Clams cooked in red curry paste with fish sauce, sugar, bell peppers, ginger, and basil.

KAW OB GOONG HOI POO
Assorted seafood in an oyster sauce, accompanied by mushrooms, vegetables, and cashews.

NAM PRIK PLA TOO
Fried mackerel with a sauce of shrimp paste, garlic, chilies, fish sauce, sugar, and lime juice.

PAD GOONG MUNG-GORN
Stir-fried lobster with ginger sauce.

PAD PED PLA DOOK
Catfish stir-fried in a spicy sauce with Thai eggplant and basil.

PLA KAPONG KEEMAO
Whole fish with a sauce of garlic, chilies, scallions, and cilantro, with lime juice, kaffir lime leaves, Thai sweet basil, sugar, and fish sauce. All the Thai ingredients seem to be here, and this has to be one of the great classic tastes to go with fish. Hot and sour, it's an incredibly light fish dish.

PLA KAPONG PAO
Red snapper baked with red curry paste, coconut milk, fish sauce, sugar, and kaffir lime leaves.

PLA KEM TAUD
Fried, sun-dried fish with chilies, lime juice, and shallots.

PLA MUK LAD PRIG
Squid stir-fried with chilies and assorted vegetables, simmered in a tamarind-chili sauce, with scallions and cilantro to garnish.

PLA MUK PAD PED
Squid marinated in a garlic/fish sauce/soy sauce/sugar combination, quickly stir-fried, and served with fresh vegetables such as lettuce, cucumbers, and cilantro.

PLA MUK PRIG PAO
Squid stir-fried with garlic-shrimp paste and chilies, with Thai sweet basil. You'll remember eating this for more than a few minutes!

PLA NEUNG KIAMBOUY
Whole fish, such as sea bass, steamed with plum pickles, lime juice, chilies, and ginger.

PLA PRIEW WAHN
Fried whole fish with tamarind-chili sauce and assorted Asian vegetables such as straw mushrooms, baby corn, and scallions, garnished with cilantro.

PLA RAD PRIK
Crispy fried whole fish served with a sauce of fish sauce, bell peppers, garlic, onions, and Thai sweet basil.

POO NEUNG
Steamed crab with a spicy sauce of garlic, chilies, cilantro, fish sauce, lime juice, and sugar. Simple, elegant, and delicious.

POO PAD TON KRATIEM
Crab stir-fried and steamed with sesame oil, garlic, leeks, fish sauce, sugar, and onions, with an egg stirred into it.

PRIG PAO SAMUI

Clams, scallops, and shrimp stir-fried with a chili-and-garlic sauce with shrimp paste overtones, and Thai sweet basil as a complement.

TOM SOM PLA TOO

Mackerel steamed in a tamarind sauce with ginger, sugar, fish sauce, and cilantro. A most appropriate sauce to contrast with the oily nature of mackerel.

Meat and Poultry Dishes

GAI PAD BAI GA-PRAO

Spicy ground chicken with chilies, green peppercorns, fish sauce, and holy basil.

GAI PAD KHING

A very simple and popular Thai dish, the chicken is stir-fried with a good amount of ginger, plus assorted vegetables such as bell peppers, mushrooms, and onions, then seasoned with fish sauce and garnished with cilantro.

GAI PAD MED MA-MUANG HIM-MA PAN

Cashew chicken, similar to the Chinese version, but using fish sauce and oyster sauce to season rather than soy sauce. A basic stir-fry that can offset spicier dishes in a meal.

GAI PAD PUCK
Chicken stir-fried with Asian vegetables and oyster sauce.

GAI PRIEW WAN
Chicken in a sweet-and-sour sauce.

GAI YANG
Marinated and grilled chicken, aromatic, not very spicy, juicy meat with crispy skin.

GAI YANG ESAN
Grilled chicken marinated in garlic, lemongrass, and cilantro.

MOO PAD KEENG
Stir-fried pork with mushrooms and vegetables. Not too spicy.

MOO PRIG PAO
A spicy pork stir-fry with the aroma of Thai sweet basil.

NUEA PAD PRIK
Generally served over rice, this tasty dish resembles its Chinese cousin but with fish sauce rather than soy sauce as the primary seasoning. Garlic, onions, and bell peppers are the vegetables, and sesame oil blends and enhances the flavors.

NUCA PAD PRIG SOD
Take it up a few notches. Beef stir-fry with the chili factor.

NUCA PAD PUCK
Basic stir-fry of beef and broccoli, with garlic and oyster sauce.

PAD PRIK KHING MOO
Crispy pork stir-fried with water spinach. Curry paste and kaffir lime leaves go beautifully with the crispy pork.

PAD TAP GAI
Stir-fried chicken livers with onion.

PET PALO
Duck steamed over water, seasoned with garlic, cilantro, and soy sauce. Like many of the milder stir-fries, *pet palo* reflects a Chinese influence on Thai cooking.

SAI GROG ESAN
Northeastern Thailand sausage made from pork and sticky rice. The sticky rice makes for an interesting texture.

TAP WAAN
Stir-fried beef liver seasoned with fish sauce, lime juice, lemongrass, chilies, and mint leaves. A delightful change of

pace from the old liver-and-bacon routine, Thai flavors brighten the liver and make it delicious.

Sweets and Beverages

DESSERT JUST ISN'T A CONCEPT in Asia the way it is in the West. After a Thai meal, the most common thing is to eat some of the fresh fruit from the incredible bounty available there. Of course, in the United States, we're constrained to what's available and it's seldom as succulent as the fruit in the tropics.

There are special occasions, however, when dessert is served. During these occasions, two desserts are seen: one of them creamy, such as a custard, and the other candylike or cakelike. These special occasions are unusual, so it's safe to say that dessert as we know it is a rare thing in Thai cuisine. But despite the lack of a dessert course, sweets are extremely popular in Thailand. Between-meal candies are eaten fondly and often, and there is a great candy-making industry in Thailand.

In a Thai restaurant in the United States, you'll probably see dessert listed, but this is to accommodate American culture. Ice cream, fried bananas or other fruits, and fruits in syrup are common. Sticky rice is often cooked with coconut milk and served with fruits such as mango or papaya. One typical sweet would be *kao niew tat,* sticky rice cakes, which might be served with some fruit. Custards of various sorts might also be offered, and they, along with sticky rice concoctions, will give you the most authentic Thai experience . . . unless you're lucky enough to get some genuine Thai candies!

The most common beverage has traditionally been tea, but iced coffee (usually made with sweetened condensed milk) has become popular in recent years. Alcoholic beverages are generally beer or whiskey distilled from rice. Thai restaurants here often have full American bars, so you can have your martini and eat Thai too!

Glossary

MEATS

Beef—*Nuea vorh*

Hua jai	Heart
Nuea khang	Flank steak
Nuea khaon	Round
Nuea rah	Fillet
Nuea son nai	Chateaubriand
Nuea sunh nai	Tenderloin
Nuea sunh ook	Sirloin
Nuea thi barh	Chuck (shoulder)
See-khong	Rib
Steak	Steak
Tubh	Liver

Lamb—*Luuk ghag*

Nahr khang	Shank
Nuea ghag	Mutton
Nuea pehr	Stew
Nuea see khong ghag	Rib chop
Nuea thi barh	Shoulder
Nuea thong rhang	Saddle
Nuea tong khrang	Loin
Nuea tud	Chop

Nuea tud tong khrang	Loin chop
Rang	Rack

Pork—Moo

Khar moo	Ham
Khar moo sodh	Fresh ham
Moo rom quam	Smoked ham
Moo se khrong	Bacon
Naem	A spicy pork sausage of northern Thailand, a favorite regional specialty
Nuea tong khrang	Loin
Rim fhee phark	Lips
Sai grok	Sausage
See-khrong	Spareribs
See-khrong yang	Barbecued spareribs

Chicken—Gai

Gai thon	Capon
Khaa	Leg
Kheng nai	Giblets, gizzard
Mar gai	Hen
Nhong	Thigh
Nong	Drumstick
Nuea ook gai	Boneless breast

Ook	Breast
Ook rah	Cutlet
Peek	Wings
Tub	Liver

Turkey—*Gai knaung*

Gai knaung bod	Ground turkey
Ook	Breast
Ook rah	Cutlet

Veal—*Luuk vorh*

Khaa	Leg
Kha-nom pang whan	Sweetbreads
Nuea khang	Shank
Nuea thi barh	Shoulder
Nuea tong krang	Loin
Nuea tud	Chop
Ook	Breast
Ook rah	Cutlet
Tai	Kidneys
Tub	Liver

Goat—*Phah*

Ahrn; rhung	Saddle
Nuea tud	Chop

Poultry—*Sad peek*

Gai farh	Pheasant
Hahn	Goose
Nook khum	Quail
Nook krajook thed	Ostrich
Nook kratha	Partridge
Nook phirab	Squab (pigeon)
Pad	Duck

Game—*Shud lahr*

Krathaig	Rabbit
Kwang	Venison
Moo	Boar
Vorh	Buffalo

SEAFOOD

Fin fish—*Kreep pharr*

Bass	Bass
Pla charham	Shark
Pla dhab	Swordfish
Pla dook	Catfish
Pla himar	Grouper
Pla jar rha med	Pompano
Pla ka pong dang	Red snapper
Pla lai	Cod
Pla nin	Tilapia
Pla salmon	Salmon

Pla sardine	Sardine
Pla ta duoa	Eel
Pla thapien	Flounder
Pla too	Mackerel, tuna
Pra krabog	Herring

Shellfish—*Arhan talay mee phea*

Goong	Shrimp
Goong kramp kram	Crayfish
Goong mung-gorn	Lobster
Goong yai	Prawn
Hoi clam	Clam
Hoi mang phu	Mussel
Hoi nang rohm	Oyster
Hoi phat	Scallop
Hoi rai	Cockle
Hoi thag	Conch
Pao hehr	Abalone
Pla muk	Cuttlefish, octopus, squid
Poo	Crab

DAIRY PRODUCTS

Cream priew	Sour cream
Ice-cream	Ice cream
Khai	Egg
Nei	Butter
Nohm	Milk

Nohm look quam aone	Nonfat milk
Nohm priew	Yogurt

VEGETABLES	
Dawk ka-lum	Cauliflower
Fahk	Winter squash
Fahk thawng	Pumpkin
Ga lum phee	Cabbage
Hawm dang	Shallot
Hawm yai	Onion
Hed	Mushroom
Hed pha	Wild mushroom
Hua chai taoe	Turnip
Hua phak kaat	Radish
Kha	Galanga root (galangal)
Kha naar	Broccoli
Khao phoht	Corn
Khao phoht onn	Baby corn
Khen chai	Celery
Kra tiam	Garlic
Makheua muang	Eggplant
Makheua thet	Tomato
Mun farang	Potato
Mun thet	Yam
Mun whan	Sweet potato
Mun-kwal	Jicama

Prik	Pepper
Prik khee knu	Hot pepper
Prik whan	Sweet pepper
Puck boong	Water spinach or water morning glory
Taeng kwaa	Cucumbers
Thua lun-tao	Snow pea
Ton hawm	Scallion
Ton kra tiam	Leek
Tua	Bean, bean sprouts
Tua dum	Black bean
Tua khak	Pinto bean
Tua khoa	White bean
Tua shod	Pea
Yherha	Fennel

FRUITS

A-ngoung	Grape
Bai mar khod	Kaffir lime leaf
Kiew hom	Banana
Lhok phub	Persimmon
Ma-fung	Star fruit
Ma-khaam	Tamarind
Ma-lakaw	Papaya
Ma-muang	Mango
Ma-nao	Lime
Ma-phrao	Coconut

Mun sum pra rung	Casaba
Phon mar khod	Kaffir lime
Som	Orange
Som kheao-wan	Tangerine
Sub-pra-rod	Pineapple
Taeng-moh	Watermelon
Thang	Melon
Tub-tim	Pomegranate

GRAINS

Khao	Rice
Khao dang	Brown rice
Khao hom ma-ree	Jasmine rice
Khao kao	White rice
Khao kate	Basmati rice
Khao phaa	Wild rice

HERBS AND SPICES

Bai ba-prao	Basil
Bai hurapa	Holy basil
Bai mang lak	Thai sweet basil
Bai saraneh	Mint
Bai tyoe	Pandanus
Dao dok chan	Star anise
Dok chan	Anise
Dok chan ted	Mace
Gaeng	Curry

Kamin	Turmeric
Khan obb chehi	Cinnamon
Khing	Ginger
Krachai	Lesser ginger
Lookh chan ted	Nutmeg
Ma-lhed prik sri chom phu	Pink peppercorn
Ma-lhed prik thai	Peppercorn
Med puck chee	Coriander seed
Mehd saraneh	Marjoram
Ngha	Sesame seed
Phonk kamin ted	Saffron
Prik	Chilies
Prik chee fah	Paprika
Prik khagh	Cayenne
Prik phon	Chili powder
Puck chee	Cilantro
Puck-chee farung	Parsley
Sui-chai	Chive
Ta-krai	Lemongrass
Yee rahh	Fennel

NUTS

Lok gua rut	Chestnut
Ma phrao	Coconut
Ma-muang him-ma pan	Cashew

Tua	Nut
Tua ar-mun	Almond
Tua lisong	Peanut
Tua mun-hoor	Walnut

MISCELLANEOUS INGREDIENTS

Barh mee	Egg noodles
Ga-thi	Coconut milk
Gher	Salt
Guew teaw	Rice noodles
Hua ga-thi	Coconut cream
Kra phi	Shrimp paste
Mar grog dam	Black olives (ripe)
Mar grog kheiw	Green olives
Nam mon	Oil
Nam mon hoi	Oyster sauce
Nam mon mar grog	Olive oil
Nam mon ngarh	Sesame oil
Nam pla	Fish sauce
Nam prik sri rachar	Tabasco sauce
Nam sauces satek	Steak sauce
Nam-som farung	Balsamic vinegar
Nam-som lao khao	Wine vinegar
Nam-som sai chu	Vinegar
Phan por pahr	Rice paper
See eiw	Soy sauce
Senh lek	Bean thread noodles

THAI CUISINE

Tao jew	Yellow bean sauce
Tau-hoo	*Tofu*
Voon senh	Cellophane noodles

SPECIAL DIETS

Jay	Vegetarian
Pharr	Allergic

Vietnamese Cuisine

VIETNAMESE CUISINE SHOWS influences from its Southeast Asian neighbors, as well as from 1,000 years of Chinese rule and 100 years of French rule. But Vietnam has managed to create a flavor and style all its own. Vietnamese food, it has been said, lies somewhere between Thai and Chinese cuisines, avoiding the extreme spiciness of Thai food and the fat of Chinese cuisine.

French influence results in the Vietnamese fondness for *café au lait*, many dairy products, and French bread. In the South, they often sauté in pans rather than stir-fry in woks. Their curries stem from Indian influence on Laos, Cambodia, and Thailand, which in turn influenced Vietnam. And many of the ingredients common to Vietnamese cuisine today, such as corn, tomatoes, potatoes, peanuts, and chilies, came from the New World via European explorers of the 1500s. Yet through it all, Vietnamese have maintained their own culinary identity.

DID YOU KNOW?

Vietnamese use chopsticks, a result of the 1,000-year Chinese rule. In Cambodia, food is eaten with the hands, and in Laos and Thailand, forks are common.

What Makes It Vietnamese: Special Ingredients In Vietnamese Cuisine

VIETNAM USES MANY of the same ingredients found in other Asian cuisines, especially those of Southeast Asia. Still, there are differences, and something like galanga root, so widely used in Thai cuisine, is rarely found in Vietnamese dishes. Familiarity with these items helps in understanding the special flavors of Vietnamese cuisine.

BAC HA
Tropical mint. A type of spearmint, used in Vietnamese salads and especially in vegetable platters.

BANH PHONG TOM
Shrimp or prawn chips, made from ground shrimp, tapioca starch, and egg whites. They're puffy, airy, and tender, with a slightly salty taste, served as a snack or an accompaniment to the meal. You'll recognize them by their pink color.

BANH TRANG
Rice papers, used to make spring rolls and to wrap grilled foods.

BI HEO KHO
Dried, shredded pork skin.

CA DE
Chinese or Asian eggplant. One of many various eggplants, this one is long and thin, devoid of the bitter taste often found in the standard European variety.

CAI XANH

Flowering Chinese cabbage. With crisp green leaves and yellow flowers, this vegetable adds a delicate taste and tender crispiness that Vietnamese cooks especially love.

CU CAI TRANG

Daikon. The famous Japanese radish, like a giant white carrot, used raw in salads or pickled.

CU DAU

Jicama. Like a very large turnip with thick brown skin, the inside has the texture of a water chestnut with very little taste, just a hint of pear. Used raw, and sometimes cooked in stir-fries.

CU KIEU CHUA

Sweet-and-sour pickled scallions, an accompaniment to various dishes.

CU NGHE

Turmeric, used in Vietnamese foods primarily as a coloring.

DAU DUA

Long beans. These are the really long ones, about a foot or two. Similar to regular green beans but especially crunchy.

DAU HAO

Oyster sauce, a common Southeast Asian condiment.

DAU ME

Sesame oil. The standard Chinese type of oil, made from roasted sesame seeds. It's used to enhance and blend flavors in stir-fries and marinades.

DAU PHONG

Peanuts, an essential ingredient in Vietnamese cuisine, often found ground up in a dipping sauce or on top of some other dish.

DAU PHU

Tofu, or bean curd. Not long ago, Chinese cookbooks always referred to this as bean curd, as did Chinese menus. Now, most Americans understand the word *tofu,* which is indeed bean curd. Made from soybeans, this white curd has all the protein you need and absorbs any flavors you give it. It has a dense, custardlike texture that is very pleasing on the palate. Most kids love it, which tells you something.

DAU XANH

Yellow mung beans, which are made by husking green mung beans. Used in starchy dishes and in sweets.

DUONG PHEN
Rock sugar, used instead of white sugar for its extra sweetness.

GAO NEP
Glutinous or sticky rice.

GIA
Bean sprouts. Mung bean sprouts, that is. They are the sprouts that were at one time the only bean sprouts you ever saw in American markets. Mostly they're used raw in Vietnamese dishes, even dishes that are cooked, unlike in Chinese food. That way, they retain their crunchy texture.

GIAM GAO
Rice vinegar.

GIO
Vietnamese pork sausage. Savory and delicious.

GUNG
Ginger root. In Vietnamese cooking, ginger is used both for its spicy flavor and its ability to mask undesirable odors.

HAT SEN
Lotus seeds. Used in stew, soups, and sweets. They resemble large peanuts.

HE

Chinese chives. They have a garlicky sub-taste, otherwise they resemble Western chives. *He* are found in *goi cuon* (fresh spring rolls) and on a *dia rau song* (vegetable platter).

HOA CHAM

Lily buds. Used in stir-fries, they're also known as golden needles. They're found extensively in Chinese stir-fries.

HOA HE

Flowering chives. Used in many soups and salads to impart a distinct and refreshing oniony taste.

HOA HOI

Star anise, the same as that used in Chinese cooking. The flavor is of licorice, much like anise seed.

HUNG LIU

Five-spice powder, the same as the Chinese version: star anise, fennel or anise seed, cloves, cinnamon, and Szechuan pepper.

KHE

Star fruit. Ripe, it tastes like a blend of kiwifruit and strawberries; unripe, it is used in salads and soups, where it can replace tamarind.

KHOAI MON

Taro root. Used in Vietnamese cooking much as a potato. Taro root is used to make *poi,* the infamous Hawaiian version of grits. In other words, it's soft and sticky when cooked, and it's good for soaking up flavors in stews.

LA CHUOI

Banana leaves. You will often find food served in banana leaves, also used for wrapping and steaming in various dishes.

LAP XUONG

Chinese sausage.

MAM NEM

Anchovy sauce. A blend of fermented anchovies with salt, this sauce as bottled is diluted to make the traditional *mam nem* dipping sauce.

MAM TOM

Shrimp sauce, a Vietnamese version of the same highly aromatic stuff used throughout Southeast Asia. There are various types of shrimp pastes and sauces, all very pungent. They add a wonderful depth of flavor along with saltiness to soups, sauces, and stir-fries.

MANG

Bamboo shoots. Familiar to most Americans because of their exposure to Chinese food.

ME

Sesame seeds, usually toasted, used to enhance dipping sauces and marinades.

ME CHUA

Tamarind, used in its sour form in soups. There are pods with seeds in them, and soaking the pulp of the pods and straining it yields a sour liquid.

MIA

Sugarcane. One particularly delicious dish using sugarcane is *cha tom,* which is shrimp paste wrapped around a sugarcane stalk and grilled. The shrimp is pulled off the sugarcane, then served with fresh vegetables and wrapped in lettuce or rice papers.

NAM HUONG

Chinese black mushrooms, essentially the dried version of *shiitake* mushrooms.

NAM NHI

Tree ear or wood ear mushrooms. A fungus that looks like a small human ear. In stir-fries they add a soft, chewy texture with very little flavor.

NAM ROM

Straw mushrooms with distinct umbrella-shaped caps. Their mild flavor and firm texture make them very desirable in stir-fries.

NUOC CHAM

Spicy fish sauce, made from *nuoc mam* (fish sauce), garlic, chilies, sugar, lime juice, and rice vinegar. Ubiquitous as a dipping sauce, served with just about everything.

NUOC CHAM HOISIN

Hoisin sauce, the Chinese sauce made of soybeans, garlic, vinegar, sesame oil, and sugar, used in barbecue sauces and dips.

NUOC DUA

Coconut milk, used in curries.

NUOC MAM

Vietnamese fish sauce, used to flavor many dishes. It is more strongly flavored than the Thai version.

OT

Chilies, from hot to fiery-hot. Known only since Europeans brought them from the New World, chilies have become an integral part of Vietnamese cuisine.

RAU HUNG QUE

Asian or Thai basil. With a distinct anise flavor, *rau hung que* is the requsite herb for *pho bo,* the famous Vietnamese beef noodle soup.

RAU MUONG

Water spinach or water morning glory. Very popular throughout Asia, it looks like spinach with small leaves, has the texture of watercress, and the taste of mild spinach.

RAU NGO/MUI

Cilantro, also known as Chinese parsley or coriander. Ubiquitous in Vietnamese food, contributing much to its characteristic flavor.

RIENG

Galanga root, a pungent cousin of ginger.

TAN XAI

Pickled Chinese cabbage, very strong and smelly. Small quantities are used in soups and noodle dishes.

THACH DEN

Grass jelly, made from seaweed and cornstarch, used in sweet drinks.

THACH TRANG

Agar-agar. A gelatin from seaweed used in *thit ga dong* (jellied chicken) and wherever gelatin is required.

THINH

Roasted rice powder, used as a flavoring and binding agent.

TINH DAU HOA

Various flower waters, used to flavor sweet beverages and desserts.

TOM KHO

Dried shrimp; used as a seasoning in soups and stir-fries, they are very strongly flavored.

TUONG

Soybean sauce, not the traditional soy sauce, but a milder-tasting sauce used especially in Vietnamese vegetarian dishes.

TUONG CA RI

Vietnamese curry paste. It is much hotter than Indian curry powders and has a different aroma.

TUONG OT TUOI

Chili paste. A table condiment similar to Tabasco but hotter, with garlic in it.

XA

Lemongrass. Like cilantro, an absolutely necessary ingredient to give Vietnamese food its characteristic flavor. Its lemony aroma is very refreshing in a light noodle soup or in a fresh salad.

XI DAU
Soy sauce.

NOODLES

Noodles are very common to Vietnamese cuisine. Rice noodles, often in the form of vermicelli (known as bun), serve as a base for many Vietnamese noodle dishes. Wheat flour- and mung bean flour-based noodle dishes are also common.

More information on these types of noodles appears in the section on Thai cuisine.

Appetizers

VIETNAMESE MEALS ARE usually served all at once, but there are many dishes that are eaten as snacks or as small parts of bigger meals. These make good appetizers in American restaurants. Also, the French influence in Vietnam made the concept of multi-course meals less strange than in other Southeast Asian countries.

BANH BOT LOC
Boiled shrimp-and-pork dumplings. The filling is seasoned with fish sauce, and the dough is made from tapioca starch. *Nuoc cham* (spicy fish sauce) is the typical dipping sauce.

BANH KHOAI MON

A truly delicious meat turnover with a crust made of taro root. The filling is made of ground pork, garlic, onion, and lemongrass, seasoned with curry, fish sauce, and sugar.

BANH MI CHIEN VOI TOM

Shrimp toast. Similar to the standard Chinese shrimp toast, but seasoned with fish sauce rather than soy sauce.

BO DUN

Grilled beef strips with bacon, threaded on a skewer and grilled. This dish is often part of a festive meal called *bo bay mon,* which includes seven beef dishes.

CHA BO

Grilled beef patties, seasoned with peanuts, coconut milk, and shallots, cooked on skewers. Good but rather uninspired, with the fish sauce coming through a little too much sometimes.

CHA GIO

Fried spring rolls, generally stuffed with mushrooms, crabmeat, shrimp, pork, vegetables, and seasonings. To eat one, wrap it in a lettuce leaf along with some ingredients from the vegetable platter, and, of course, dip it in *nuoc cham* (spicy fish sauce). Another popular way to serve spring rolls is cut into pieces, served on top of vegetables and noodles in individual bowls, and topped with chopped peanuts and *nuoc cham*.

CHA GIO TOM

Fried shrimp rolls, made with whole shrimp, along with beef, pork, and crabmeat, all wrapped in rice paper.

CUON DIEP

Lettuce rolls. Very similar to fresh spring rolls, but the wrapper is a lettuce leaf.

GOI CUON

Fresh spring rolls. Rice paper is used as the wrapper, and the filling is basically a Vietnamese salad with cooked pork and shrimp. A fresh spring roll is not fried.

MUC CHIEN

Squid, coated with cornstarch and fried. Another fine way to enjoy this delightful seafood. The dipping sauce is—you guessed it—*nuoc cham*.

MUC TUOI NUONG

Griddled squid, marinated in garlic and fish sauce. Garnished with cilantro, this is a simple and delicious way to serve squid. Cooked at a high heat, the squid stays moist and tender.

Salads

SALAD MAKES UP AN important part of Vietnamese food. The vegetable platter described below is absolutely essential to the cuisine, and other fresh salads are an enjoyable aspect of Vietnamese food.

BO LUC LAC

Warm, sautéed beef tossed with lettuce and watercress, dressed with a garlic-and-onion vinaigrette. The marinated beef (garlic, sugar, soy sauce, fish sauce) contrasts nicely with the crisp, refreshing salad greens and the light dressing.

DIA RAU SONG

Vegetable platter. The vegetable platter is ubiquitous in Vietnamese meals. Its array of fresh vegetables and fruits is used to wrap cooked foods at the table. While not a salad as such, it is included here because, like other salads, it epitomizes the Vietnamese love of fresh produce. Typical ingredients are lettuce leaves, sliced cucumbers, cilantro, mint, scallions, mung bean sprouts, and basil. Fresh pickled scallions or cucumbers are also possible. The vegetable platter is yet another example of the Vietnamese combination of cooked food with raw vegetables, a real taste and texture treat for western palates tired of too much meat and rich sauces.

GA XE PHAY

Chicken and cabbage salad. A very popular salad in Vietnam. Cabbage, chicken, carrots, and mint are all shredded and mixed together with a hot-sweet-sour dressing.

GOI BAP CHUOI

Banana blossoms with chicken in a typical sweet-and-sour dressing, garnished with cilantro and chopped peanuts.

GOI BO

Beef salad with roasted rice powder. A nice, zingy dish. Roasted rice powder is simply pan-roasted rice ground up into powder, used as a flavor enhancer especially on salads.

GOI DU DU

Green papaya salad, with grilled dried beef, carrots, and cilantro, all julienned and mixed with a light hot-sweet-sour dressing. Generally served with sticky rice.

GOI GA

Chicken-and-grapefruit salad with shredded cabbage, carrots, and herbs.

GOI MUC

Squid salad with tamarind; the tamarind gives the salad its distinctive tart flavor.

GOI NAM TRANG

Vegetable, pork, and shrimp salad, with a light and spicy dressing. Omelette strips, seen in several dishes, are included.

GOI TOM THIT

A standard, with pork and shrimp tossed with carrots, celery, onions, and cucumbers with a light, refreshing dressing.

NOM TRAI BUOI

A beautiful salad of chicken, pork sausage, shrimp, cucumbers, bean sprouts, carrots, omelette strips, grapefruit, and sesame seeds. Dressed with the standard hot-sweet-sour dressing, garnished with ground peanuts and cilantro, and served with shrimp chips.

RAU MUONG TRON

Water spinach salad, with a basic dressing.

RAU TRON

Mixed beans, such as black-eyed peas, black beans, or white beans, with pork and a spicy dressing.

Soups

VIETNAMESE SOUPS VARY widely and are included in most meals. Breakfast includes a *pho*, or *bun* (noodle soup). Soup may be an entire lunch, a snack, or the prelude to a bigger meal. Regardless of when they're served, Vietnamese soups deserve their legendary status as flavor "monsters."

PHO OR BUN

Noodle soup. *Pho* means "your own bowl," because noodle soups are served in each person's bowl, rather than on the platters of food shared by everyone. *Pho* is the traditional breakfast in Vietnam, but it is also eaten throughout the day in soup stalls. *Pho* is broth with meat and/or seafood, as well as either rice or egg noodles of various sizes. It also contains fresh, cold bean sprouts, herb sprigs, chilies, scallions, lime wedges, preserved cabbage, and possibly other vegetables. Lemongrass often plays a part. The contrast between cold and warm, and cooked and raw, demonstrates precisely and beautifully the essence of Vietnamese cuisine. The heat level is nowhere near as high as that in many Thai dishes. It's just enough to cause some perspiring about halfway through the dish, which creates a wonderful cooling sensation in the tropical heat. It also clears the head and lungs. *Pho* is the absolute epitome of comfort food. It heals the body and spirit alike. Enjoy!

BUN RIEU

Crab dumpling and rice vermicelli soup. When made in the authentic way, crab roe is added, which imparts a rich pungency to the soup.

BUN THANG

Rice vermicelli soup with sausage, pork, shrimp, and chicken (or other combinations of meat and seafood). Strips of thin, plain omelette are also added. The soup is seasoned with fish sauce, and chilies, lime, and shrimp sauce are served on the side.

CANH GIO VIEN

Meatball soup.

CANH CAI GA

Chicken and mustard-cabbage soup, very delicate.

CANH CU CAI

Daikon and pork soup.

CANH DAU PHU HE

Pork, *tofu,* and Chinese chive bud soup.

CANH RAU MUONG THIT BO

Water spinach and beef soup. The beef is marinated in the typical sauce of garlic, shallots, sugar, and fish sauce.

CANH THIT BO NAU DUA

Beef and pineapple soup, with tomatoes and onions.

CANH TOM CHUA

Hot-and-sour shrimp soup, with tomatoes, pineapple, bamboo shoots, bean sprouts, and fresh chilies. Two special ingredients are in the authentic version of this soup: *ngo om* (rice paddy herb), a sour herb, and the spongy stem from *rau doc mung,* a type of aquatic plant.

CANH TRUNG CA CHUA
Tomato and egg drop soup, in a chicken stock.

CHAO THIT BO
Rice and beef soup, garnished with ground peanuts, cilantro, and scallions.

HU TIEU
A chicken broth poured over chicken, shrimp, pork, and vegetables, which are piled over noodles. Serving the broth on the side allows each diner to control the ration of liquid to garnish. An adaptation of a Chinese concept, *hu tieu* is a very flavorful concoction and not spicy at all.

MANG TAY NAU CUA
Asparagus and crabmeat soup, in a chicken broth.

MIEN GA
Chicken and cellophane (bean thread) noodle soup, spiced with fish sauce, ginger, and preserved vegetables.

PHO BAC
Beef and rice noodle soup.

PHO BO

Beef noodle soup. Originating in Hanoi, *pho bo* is considered by many to be the finest of the noodle dishes in Southeast Asia. The delicate broth goes very well with the beef, cilantro, lime, chilies, and Thai sweet basil. And the fresh bean sprouts add a great texture.

PHO CA VIEN

Fish ball noodle soup.

PHO GA

Chicken noodle soup. Almost as popular in Vietnam as beef noodle soup, *pho ga* is a comfort food *extraordinaire*. The lime garnish is a natural with chicken stock, and the spicy chilies enhance the natural cleansing sense inherent in chicken soup. This is a chicken soup for all times.

PHO TOM

Shrimp noodle soup.

PHO VIT QUAY

Roast duck noodle soup.

PHO XA XIU

Barbecued pork noodle soup.

SUP BAP GA

Chicken and corn soup in a pork stock, light and flavorful.

Seafood

BOTH FRESH- AND SALTWATER FISH and seafood are important in Vietnamese cuisine. Vietnam enjoys 1,400 miles of
coastline, and inland areas have developed freshwater aqua-
culture to raise carp, perch, frogs, crabs, and shrimp. No
other cuisine features a greater variety of seafood.

BANH TOM

Shrimp and sweet-potato cakes, deep-fried, and served with
lettuce leaves and a vegetable platter.

CA CHIEN

Crispy red snapper with spicy tomato sauce. A great sauce
for this hearty fish, and a typical Vietnamese flavor, is derived from garlic, tomatoes, fish sauce, sugar, cilantro, and
scallions.

CA CHIEN XOT CA CHUA

Fried fish steaks in tomato sauce, a simple treatment for any
fish cut in steaks.

CA HAP

Steamed whole fish with tiger lilies. Whole fish is a sign of celebration in Vietnamese cooking, and the more garnishes, the bigger the celebration! This one has assorted vegetables and just enough kick to help purify the blood, and is served with cellophane noodles.

CA HAP VOI TOM SO

Steamed trout stuffed with a paste of shrimp and scallops. The trout found in Vietnam is milder than the American variety, but this treatment works extremely well not only with trout but with any American freshwater fish.

CA KHO TO

Fish in a clay pot, topped with a caramel–*nuoc mam* sauce over the fish, simply baked. The sauce includes shallots and chilies that enhance the flavor of the fish.

CA NUONG LA CHUOI

Grilled fish wrapped in a banana leaf, a traditional cooking method that helps concentrate the flavors of the shallots, garlic, chilies, and whatever else is included in the packet.

CA NUONG VI

Tuna with dill and toasted almonds, grilled.

CA NUONG XA OT

Grilled fish with lemongrass and chilies, a delicious way to cook any fish, but especially suited to the more oily varieties.

CA RAN

Deep-fried flounder, served with *nuoc cham* for dipping.

CA RANG CHUA NGOT

Sweet-and-sour fish.

CHA CA HA NOI

A traditional dish from Hanoi, generally cooked at the table. Marinated fish is stir-fried with dill, scallions, and peanuts, and served over vermicelli.

CHA MUC

Squid cakes with dill, fried and tasty.

CUA RANG MUOI

Fried crab, a very simple dish eaten in casual settings. In Vietnam, freshwater crabs are used. Over here, any available crab is okay.

ECH KHO XA OT

Frog legs cooked with chilies and lemongrass.

ECH XAO LAN

Frog legs in a Southeast Asian curry with garlic, curry paste, chilies, lemongrass, fish sauce, coconut milk, and peanuts. You were always told that frog legs tasted like chicken, and here's a style that really makes them taste that way!

HAI SAN XAO RAU

Stir-fried seafood with mixed vegetables and basil. A typical Southern Vietnamese stir-fry, with a nod to the Chinese influence. Mildly spicy, but very flavorful with garlic, fish sauce, and oyster sauce.

MUC DON

Stuffed squid. The stuffing is the tentacles of the squid, cellophane noodles, tree ears, tomatoes, and onions. The dish is sautéed and served with *nuoc mam ngo* (cilantro-chili sauce) on the side. For the squid fans out there, this is a fantastic dish.

MUC XAO CAI CHUA

Stir-fried squid with pickled mustard greens, a nice taste and texture contrast.

TOM CANG NUONG

Grilled shrimp, with a dip of *nuoc cham* or lime juice with salt and pepper.

TOM CHIEN BOT

Batter-fried shrimp, very much the same thing as the Chinese version, served with a sweet-and-sour sauce.

TOM HUM SAI GON

A Southern-style lobster curry, creamy and not necessarily very spicy.

TOM NUONG VI

Curried shrimp. The curry spices are stuffed into the shell, then the shrimp is grilled, removed from the shell, and eaten. Very spicy—eat with plenty of rice!

TOM RIM

Caramelized shrimp. A fiery-hot and sweet dish with plenty of garlic, a wonderful treatment for shrimp.

Meats

IN VIETNAM, THE MOST POPULAR meat by far is pork, both because it's tasty and because it's quite cheap to raise. Beef, which requires extensive grazing space, has traditionally been very expensive there, so its use has been reserved more for special occasions, like *bo bay mon,* a special seven-course beef meal served in specialty restaurants. It is also cooked at home for special occasions. The meal always starts with *bo nhung giam* (beef fondue with vinegar). The next five dishes are *cha dum* (steamed beef pâté), *goi bo* (warm beef salad), *bo nuong la nho* (stuffed grape leaves), *bo dun* (beef skewered with bacon), and *cha bo* (grilled beef patties). The meal ends with *chao thit bo* (beef and rice soup).

BANH HOI THIS NUONG
Grilled pork with noodle cakes. A classic dish. The *banh hoi* (noodle cakes) are a nice way to eat vermicelli. Basically, the pasta is steamed into a cake and cut into pieces.

BANH UOT THIS NUONG
Barbecued beef wrapped in fresh rice papers. A typical barbecue marinade includes lemongrass, garlic, sugar, shallots, fish sauce, sesame seeds, and sesame oil.

BE THUI
Vietnamese roast beef with ginger sauce. A traditional Northern specialty, the sliced beef is served with lettuce

leaves and a vegetable platter, plus noodles. Each person makes a lettuce wrap and dips it in a ginger sauce.

BO NHUNG DAM

Beef in vinegar sauce, a classic dish from the South. The sauce is coconut juice (or coconut water) and rice vinegar, with sugar and garlic. One of the seven dishes of the *bo bay mon* feast.

BO NUONG XA

Grilled beef with lemongrass, served with lettuce leaves. Each leaf is then filled by the diner with a piece of the beef and items from a vegetable platter.

BO XAO LAN

Beef curry. The flavor of Vietnamese curry resembles Chinese five-spice powder with the addition of chilies for heat. *Hot mau,* from the red-colored nut of a Vietnamese tree, is added for a deep red color. Vietnamese curry is quite distinct from the yellow curry of India. Also, as in Thai curries, coconut milk is standard. Lemongrass adds a nice subtle citrus background. And *voilà!*

BUN CHA

Grilled pork with rice vermicelli. The dish is either served as a noodle dish or with a vegetable platter and lettuce leaves.

BUN THIT NUONG

Barbecued pork with rice noodles. A standard marinade for barbecued pork contains shallots, garlic, sugar, and fish sauce.

If *Bun thit nuong* is served in the traditional manner, you'll get one bowl with the pork garnished with peanuts and scallions, and another bowl with noodles. From a vegetable platter you take what you like and add it to the noodles, then put small amounts from the pork bowl over the noodles. You eat from the noodle bowl.

CHA DUM

Steamed beef pâté, which is wrapped in banana leaves, and served with *banh da nuoc dua nuong* (grilled coconut rice paper).

CHA LUA

Vietnamese pork sausage, usually cut into small pieces, and always served cold.

CHA TRUNG

Ground pork-and-egg cake, sort of like *egg foo yung,* or a very thick omelette.

HU TIEU AP CHAO

Pork and shrimp stir-fried with noodles. Chili flakes add zest and a garnish of chopped peanuts enhances the Vietnamese character of this dish, but the technique and overall flavor resembles a Chinese stir-fry.

MAM HAP

Steamed pork loaf, basic and tasty.

NEM NUONG

Skewered meatballs, a specialty of the central region of Vietnam. The seasoning is subtle, and the meatballs are served with rice papers and a vegetable platter, so you can roll everything up in a neat package, dip in a delightful peanut sauce, and enjoy.

SUON NUONG

Barbecued spareribs, with a marinade of caramel sauce, lemongrass, shallots, garlic, and chilies. A nice break from standard Chinese-style ribs.

THIT BO RANG RUOC SA

Ground beef with lemongrass and shrimp sauce. The shrimp sauce blends in well in this stir-fry, although it does make its presence known.

THIT BO XAO BONG CAI NAM VANG
Stir-fried beef and cauliflower with mushrooms.

THIT BO XAO CAN
Stir-fried beef with celery.

THIT BO XAO KHOAI TAY
Beef with french fries, but with a twist. The Vietnamese first fry the potatoes, then stir-fry them with the beef and vegetables. The potatoes get soggy, but they absorb all of the nice Vietnamese flavors.

THIT BO XAO OT XANH
Stir-fried beef with green peppers and broccoli, much like a Chinese stir-fry, but with the ubiquitous *nuoc mam* in place of soy sauce.

THIT HEO XOT CA CHUA
Ground pork in tomato sauce, with *nuoc mam,* garlic, cilantro, and mint. The thick sauce is served over rice and a bed of shredded lettuce. *Nuoc cham* is served on the side.

THIT KHO NUOC DUA
Pork cooked with coconut water, seasoned with fish sauce sweetened with caramel.

Poultry

CHICKEN IS LESS COMMON in Vietnamese cooking than in American cooking, mostly because poultry is generally more expensive than pork.

CANH GA KHO GUNG
Chicken wings in caramel sauce and ginger.

GA CA RI
Curried chicken, usually includes potatoes, onions, tomatoes, and carrots, all in a coconut-milk sauce. The dish is similar to other Southeast Asian curries but is usually less fiery.

GA HAP GIAM-BONG
Chicken steamed with ham and Chinese cabbage. A dish that shows French influence on Vietnamese cooking, although the seasonings are typically Vietnamese.

GA KHO
"Singing chicken," a very hot stir-fry guaranteed to spice up your life.

GA NUONG SA
Roast chicken with lemongrass.

GA XAO
Fried chicken with broccoli, in which the chicken is deep-fried and mixed with stir-fried vegetables.

GA XAO DUA HANH NHAN

Chicken with pineapple and cashews. A stir-fried dish with Vietnamese character and some zing from chilies.

GA XE PHAY

Shredded chicken with mint, a cold dish.

LONG GA XAO GUNG

Stir-fried chicken giblets with ginger.

THIT GA KHO GUNG

Simmered chicken with ginger, a specialty from Central Vietnam.

THIT GA NAU DONG

Jellied chicken, a Northern Vietnamese dish that is generally accompanied by pickled mustard greens.

THIT GA XAO DAM GUNG SA

Fried chicken with vinegar and lemongrass.

VIT BO LO

Lacquered duck, generally served over noodles. The marinade is a sweet, salty, five-spice mixture, which gives a beautiful finish to the duck.

VIT QUAY

Barbecued roast duck. A typical marinade includes garlic, ginger, coriander seeds, five-spice powder, cinnamon, star anise, and honey.

VIT TIEM MIA

Duck coated with sliced sugarcane and simmered with coconut water and nuts. A different approach to duck, and very tasty.

Vegetarian Dishes

VIETNAM HAS A LONG TRADITION of vegetarian cooking from the Buddhists who came from China. Most Vietnamese who are Buddhist aren't strict vegetarians, although Buddhist monks are. Nonetheless, a large number of Vietnamese observe vegetarian days that have spiritual meaning, and vegetarian dishes are invariably served as part of a meal.

Tofu is an extremely important vegetarian food both because of its protein content and its versatility.

Interestingly, strict Buddhist vegetarians don't eat garlic or onions, which are considered stimulating and thus unholy. Leeks, on the other hand, are used frequently.

BAP CAI XAO BUN TAU

Stir-fried cabbage and *tofu* with cellophane noodles.

BI CHAY

Fried vegetables with noodles, usually rice vermicelli.

BONG CAI XAO NAM ROM

Stir-fried leeks, cauliflower, and straw mushrooms.

CA DE TAM BOT

Batter-fried eggplant.

COM CHAY

Buddha rice, a Vietnamese tradition. *Com chay* is eaten on certain religious days. It is essentially ginger-infused rice cooked in coconut milk.

DAU PHU VA LA GHEM NUONG VI

Grilled *tofu* and vegetables.

DAU PHU XAO DAU

Stir-fried *tofu* with green beans.

DAU PHU XAO LAN

Curried *tofu,* in the coconut milk style of Southeast Asia.

DAU PHU XAO THAP CAM

Stir-fried *tofu* stewed with tomatoes, peppers, eggplant, squash, and mushrooms.

GOI CHAY

Carrot, jicama, and *tofu* salad.

GOI DAU PHU

Fried *tofu* salad, in which the *tofu* is sautéed and mixed with carrots, celery, and cucumbers in a light and spicy dressing.

KIEM

Winter-squash and sweet-potato stew with coconut and peanuts. A mild stew, very comforting in the winter.

RAU MUONG XAO TOI

Stir-fried water spinach with garlic. A favorite Vietnamese vegetable dish.

RAU XAO CHAY

Lemongrass and vegetable stir-fry.

Desserts and Beverages

LIKE MOST OF ASIA, Vietnam doesn't have a strong dessert tradition. After a meal, Vietnamese most commonly eat fruit, which grows in abundance in Southeast Asia. Sweets are available, but they are consumed more as snacks than as desserts.

Unlike most of Asia, however, Vietnam enjoys a great deal of coffee, a leftover from the time of French rule. While the French pastry shops have gone, coffee has stayed popular. The most common way to drink it is with sweetened condensed milk. The coffee is dark roasted, much like French coffee, and usually prepared in a small drip pot, one cup at a time.

Tea is also very popular. Black and green teas are the two most common types. Special varieties enjoyed by Vietnamese are jasmine, which is light, flowery, and mild, and artichoke tea, generally sweetened with honey.

The two alcoholic beverages most commonly consumed are rice wine, of which there are many types, and a strong vetch distilled from glutinous rice. Beer and other spirits are also popular.

Glossary

MEATS

Beef—*Thit bo*

De suon	Rib
Gan	Liver
Thit bap dui	Round
Thit bo bit tet hao hang	Porterhouse
Thit nac vai	Flank steak
Thit non	Chateaubriand
Thit non bo	Tenderloin
Thit than	Fillet
Thit than suon	Sirloin
Thit vai	Steak
Thit vai co xuong	Chuck (shoulder)
Tim	Heart

Lamb—*Cuu*

De suon	Rib chop
Khuc thit giua lung	Saddle
Tang suon	Rack
Thit cuu	Mutton
Thit cuu ham	Stew
Thit lung	Loin
Thit lung sat suon	Loin chop
Thit vai co xuong	Chop

Vai	Shoulder
Xuong ong chan	Shank

Pork—*Thit heo*

Bi heo	Pork skin
Giam bong	Ham
Gio	Vietnamese sausage
Lap xuong	Chinese sausage
Moi	Lips
Suon heo da loc thit	Spareribs
Suon heo nuong	Barbecued spareribs
Thit heo muoi	Bacon
Thit lung	Loin
Thit mong	Fresh ham
Thit mong heo hun khoi	Smoked ham
Thit vai co xuong	Chop
Xuc xich	Sausage

Chicken—*Ga*

Canh ga	Wings
Chan ga	Leg
Co, canh ga	Giblets
Dui ga	Drumstick, thigh
Ga mai	Hen
Ga trong thien	Capon
Gan	Liver

Luon ga	Breast
Me ga	Gizzard
Mon cot-let	Cutlet
Thit than	Boneless breast

Turkey—*Ga tay*

Luon ga	Breast
Mon ga tay cot-let	Cutlet
Thit ga tay xay	Ground turkey

Veal—*Thit be*

Bau duc	Kidneys
Chan	Leg
Gan	Liver
Lat thit suon	Cutlet
Thit lung	Loin
Thit than	Breast
Thit vai co xuong	Chop
Uc be	Sweetbreads
Vai	Shoulder
Xuong ong chan	Shank

Goat—*De*

Khuc thit giua lung	Saddle
Thit vai co xuong	Chop

VIETNAMESE CUISINE

Poultry—*Gia cam*

Chim bo cau	Squab (pigeon)
Chim cut	Quail
Da dieu	Ostrich
Ga go	Partridge
Ga loi	Pheasant
Ngong	Goose
Vit	Duck

Game—*Thu san*

Lon loi duc	Boar
Thit huou, nai	Venison
Tho	Rabbit
Trau	Buffalo

SEAFOOD

Fin fish—*Dong vat co vay*

Ca bon	Flounder, sole
Ca bon luoi ngua	Halibut
Ca bon than det	Turbot
Ca chi do	Red snapper
Ca choi Nam My	Wahoo
Ca day	John Dory
Ca duoi	Monkfish
Ca efin	Haddock
Ca heo	Mahimahi
Ca hoi	Salmon
Ca hoi trang	Trout

Ca hong o-xtray-lia	Orange roughy
Ca kiem	Swordfish
Ca map	Shark
Ca minh thai	Pollock
Ca moi	Sardine
Ca mu	Grouper
Ca ngu	Tuna
Ca nuc	Pompano
Ca nuc xanh	Bluefish
Ca ro	Perch
Ca tam	Sturgeon
Ca thai duong Chau Phi	Tilapia
Ca thu	Mackerel
Ca trang	Whitefish
Ca tre	Catfish
Ca trich	Herring
Ca trich day minh	Shad
Ca tuyet	Cod
Ca tuyet con	Scrod
Ca vuoc	Bass
Ca vuoc bien den	Black sea bass
Luon	Eel

Shellfish—*Dong vat co vo*

Bach tuoc	Octopus
Bao ngu	Abalone

Con diep	Scallop
Con hau	Oyster
Con trai	Mussel
Cua	Crab
Hen	Clam
Muc	Cuttlefish
Muc ong	Squid
Oc xa cu	Conch
So	Cockle
Tom	Shrimp
Tom dong	Crayfish
Tom hum	Lobster
Tom pandan	Prawn

DAIRY PRODUCTS

Bo	Butter
Bo sua trau long	Ghee
Bo tinh che	Clarified butter
Kem	Cream, ice cream
Kem danh bong	Whipped cream
Kem mieng	Clotted cream
Kem sua chua	Sour cream
Kem tuoi	Crème fraîche
Macgarin	Margarine
Nuoc sua	Buttermilk
Sua	Milk
Sua chua	Yogurt

Sua con 50% kem	Half-and-half
Sua khong kem	Nonfat milk
Sua nguyen kem	Whole milk
Trung	Egg

VEGETABLES

Bap cai	Cabbage
Bi ngo	Pumpkin
Bi xanh	Summer squash, zucchini
Bong cai	Cauliflower
Bong cai tay	Broccoli
Ca chua	Tomato
Ca chua bi	Tomatillo
Ca de	Chinese or Asian eggplant
Ca rot	Carrot
Ca tim	Eggplant
Cai bruxen	Brussels sprouts
Cai xanh	Flowering Chinese cabbage
Cai xoan	Chinese cabbage, kale
Can tay	Celery
Cay atiso	Artichoke
Cay chua me dat	Sorrel
Cay cu cai	Rutabaga
Cay tay tien	Nopales
Cu cai	Swiss chard
Cu cai do	Radish, turnip
Cu cai duong	Beet

Cu cai trang	*Daikon*
Cu cai vang	Parsnip
Cu dau	Jicama
Cu tu; khoai mo	Yam
Dau den	Black bean
Dau dua	Long bean
Dau Ha Lan	Pea
Dau lua	Kidney bean
Dau rang	Pinto bean
Dau trang	Snow pea, white bean
Dau xanh	Mung bean, yellow mung bean
Dua chuot	Cucumber
Gia	Bean sprouts
Hanh cu	Onion
Hanh la	Scallion
He tay	Shallot
Ho tieu	Pepper
Hoa cham	Lily buds
Khoai lang	Sweet potato
Khoai mon; khoai so	Taro root
Khoai tay	Potato
Mang	Bamboo shoots
Mang tay	Asparagus
Mu tac	Mustard
Nam	Mushroom
Nam cuc	Truffle
Nam dai	Wild mushroom

Nam huong	*Shiitake* or black mushroom
Nam nhi	Tree ear mushroom
Nam rom	Straw mushroom
Ngo	Corn
Ngo non	Baby corn
Ot cay	Hot pepper
Qua bi	Winter squash
Qua dau	Bean
Rau bina	Spinach
Rau boc-choi	Bok choy
Rau can	Celery root (celeriac)
Rau muong	Water spinach or water morning glory
Rau non	Baby vegetable
Rieng	Galanga root (galangal)
Su hao	Kohlrabi
Thia la	Fennel
Toi	Garlic
Toi tay	Leek
Trai bo	Avocado
Trai ot ngot	Sweet pepper

FRUITS

Anh dao	Cherry
Buoi	Grapefruit
Cam	Orange
Cay dai hoang	Rhubarb

Cay nam viet quat	Cranberry
Cha la	Date
Chanh la cam	Kaffir lime
Chanh vang	Lemon
Chanh vo xanh	Lime
Chuoi	Banana
Dao	Peach
Dau tay	Strawberry
Du du	Papaya
Dua	Coconut
Dua bo ruot xanh	Honeydew
Dua hau	Watermelon
Dua ruot do	Cantaloupe
Dua tay	Melon
Dua tho nhi ky	Casaba
Khe	Star fruit
La chanh	Kaffir lime leaf
La chuoi	Banana leaves
Le	Pear
Le gai	Prickly pear
Luu	Pomegranate
Man	Plum
Me chua	Tamarind
Mo	Apricot
Nho	Grape
Nho nam my	Passion fruit
Qua cren-so	Crenshaw

Qua hong vang	Persimmon
Qua kivi	Kiwifruit
Qua mam xoi	Blackberry, raspberry
Qua moc qua	Quince
Qua mong	Berry
Qua sung; qua va	Fig
Qua viet quat	Blueberry
Qua xuan dao	Nectarine
Quat	Kumquat
Quit	Tangerine
Tao	Apple
Xoai	Mango

GRAINS

Bot ngu coc bac phi	Couscous
Chao Italia	Polenta
Chao ngo; banh duc ngo	Hominy
Do an che tu ngo	Cornmeal
Gao lut	Brown rice
Gao nep	Sticky or glutinous rice
Gao thom; com thom	Jasmine rice
Gao thom hat dai	Basmati rice
Gao trang; com trang	White rice
Hat san	Grits
Kieu mach	Buckwheat

Kieu yen mach	Kasha
Lua hoang	Wild rice
Lua mach	Barley
Lua mi	Wheat
Lua mi tho nhi ky	Bulgur
Mi ong	Pasta
Thoc; gao; com	Rice
Yen mach	Oats

HERBS AND SPICES

Bac ha	Tropical mint
Bot ca ri	Curry
Cay bac ha	Mint
Cay bach dau khau	Cardamom
Cay bach hoa	Capers
Cay bach xu	Juniper
Cay carum	Caraway
Cay co dong nam a	Pandanus
Cay hung	Holy basil
Cay huong thao	Rosemary
Cay kinh gioi	Marjoram
Cay mui tay	Parsley
Cay ngai dam	Tarragon
Cay ngai dang	Sage
Cay nguyet que	Bay leaf
Co ca ri	Fenugreek
Co xa huong	Thyme

Cu nghe	Turmeric
Dinh huong	Clove
Gung	Ginger
Gung cu nho	Lesser ginger
Hat anh tuc	Poppy seed
Hat mu tac	Mustard seed
Hat mui	Coriander seed
Hat nhuc dau khau	Nutmeg
Hat sen	Lotus seeds
Hat tieu	Peppercorn
Hat tieu gia-mai-ca	Allspice
Hat tieu hong	Pink peppercorn
He	Chinese chives
Hoa he	Flowering chives
Hoa hoi	Star anise
Hoa oai huong	Lavender
Hoi	Anise
Hung chanh	Lemon basil
Hung liu	Five-spice powder
Hung que	Basil
Huong lieu nhuc dau khau	Mace
Kinh gioi tay	Oregano
La thom	Chives
Me	Sesame seed
Nghe tay	Saffron
Nguyet que	Laurel

Ot	Chilies
Ot bot	Chili powder
Ot cayen	Cayenne
Ot cua ga	Paprika
Que	Cinnamon
Rau hung	Savory
Rau hung que	Thai or Asian basil
Rau ngo	Chervil
Rau ngo; rau mui	Cilantro
Rieng	Galanga root (galangal)
Thia la	Dill, fennel
Thia la Ai-cap	Cumin
Xa	Lemongrass

NUTS

Dau phong	Peanut
Dua	Coconut
Hanh nhan	Almond
Hat de	Chestnut
Hat dieu	Cashew
Hat ho tran	Pistachio
Hat ma-ca-dam	Macadamia nut
Hat oc cho	Walnut
Hat thong	Pine nut
Qua ho dao pecan	Pecan
Qua phi	Hazelnut

MISCELLANEOUS INGREDIENTS

Banh phong tom	Shrimp chips
Banh trang	Rice paper
Bun; pho	Rice noodles
Bun tau	Cellophane noodles
Cu cai trang cay	Horseradish
Cu kieu chua	Sweet-and-sour pickled scallions
Dau	Oil
Dau ca-no-la	Canola oil
Dau hao	Oyster sauce
Dau me	Sesame oil
Dau o luu	Olive oil
Dau phu	*Tofu*
Duong phen	Rock sugar
Giam	Vinegar
Giam gao	Rice vinegar
Giam ruou	Wine vinegar
Giam thom	Balsamic vinegar
Mam nem	Anchovy sauce
Mam tom	Shrimp paste, shrimp sauce
Me chua	Tamarind
Mi trung	Egg noodles
Mia	Sugarcane
Mien	Bean thread noodles
Mu tac	Mustard
Muoi	Salt
Nuoc cham hoisin	*Hoisin* sauce

Nuoc cot dua	Coconut cream
Nuoc dua	Coconut milk
Nuoc mam	Fish sauce
Nuoc uop thit nuong	Steak sauce
Nuoc xot ca chua	Ketchup
Nuoc xot cay vung Uo-se-sto	Worcestershire sauce
Nuoc xot hat tieu	Hot pepper sauce
Qua o luc vang	Green olives
Qua o luu den	Black olives (ripe)
Tan xai	Pickled Chinese cabbage
Thach den	Grass jelly
Thach trang	Agar-agar
Thinh	Roasted rice powder
Tinh dau hoa	Flower water
Tom kho	Dried shrimp
Tuong	Yellow bean sauce
Tuong ca ri	Curry paste
Tuong ot tuoi	Chili paste
Xi dau	Soy sauce

SPECIAL DIETS

Benh di ung	Allergy
Benh di ung bot mi	Wheat allergy
Bi di ung	Allergic
Co it calo	Low-calorie
Co it chat beo	Low-fat

Co it muoi	Low-sodium
Co nhieu chat xo	High-fiber
Khong co bot mi	Wheat/gluten free
Khong co chat beo	Nonfat
Khong co duong	Sugar free
Khong co sua	Dairy free
Kieng an do sua	Lactose intolerant
Lam tang tuoi tho	Macrobiotic
Nguoi an chay; an chay	Vegetarian
Nguoi an chay chat che	Vegan
Nguoi an chay co dung sua va trung; an chay co dung sua va trung	Lacto-ovo vegetarian
Nguoi an chay co dung sua; an chay co dung sua	Lacto vegetarian
Nguoi chi an trai cay	Fruitarian

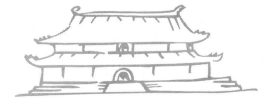

Korean Cuisine

IF YOUR FIRST THOUGHT when you think of Korean food is *kimchi,* that's okay, but read on. *Kimchi*—pickled vegetables, meat, or fish—is perhaps the best-known dish of Korea, and it is unique among Asian dishes. Indeed, *kimchi* is virtually the national dish of Korea. But there are many other foods that set Korean cuisine apart from its Asian neighbors. *Bulgogi* (barbecued beef), *galbi* (barbecued beef rib) and *jeongol* (meat and vegetable hot pot) are wildly popular and distinctly Korean dishes. The ancient cuisine of Korea has a flavor and presentation surprisingly different from the foods of its nearest neighbors, Japan and China, and it is gaining a lot of popularity in the United States.

Rice is the staple food of Korea, no surprise in Asia. Medium-grain rice that tends to hold together is the norm, making it easier to pick up with chopsticks. The blandness of steamed rice counters the highly seasoned foods that accompany it, toning down their intense flavors. Large bowls of rice are served with every meal, and several side dishes—*banchan*—complete the meal.

Following the usual Asian practice, Koreans recognize five flavors—salty, sweet, hot, bitter, and sour. Balancing the five flavors, as well as the five colors of green, white, red, yellow, and black, is a goal for Korean cooks. Any meal, then, becomes a sort of aspiration to the aesthetic, and Koreans are justly proud of the tasty, appealing results. Chopsticks and soup spoons are the only eating utensils, so Korean food is served already cut into bite-size pieces.

TIP! . . . KOREAN TABLE MANNERS

Slurping your food is the correct Korean way to eat. No one can scold you if you're in a Korean restaurant! However, blowing your nose at the table shows dreadfully bad manners. Belching during the meal is not acceptable either.

Korean cuisine is more than 2,000 years old and has developed very much in its own way. There was obvious interaction with Chinese (the original Koreans came from Mongolia), but most Korean dishes don't descend directly from Chinese cuisine. Culinary exchanges also took place during the Japanese occupation of Korea. As a result, there is Korean influence in Japanese cuisine, as well as Japanese influence in Korean cuisine (for instance, the Korean use of the Japanese "hot pot.")

The various condiments and seasonings used are common throughout Asia, but Koreans have developed their own ratios to create a distinctive Korean taste. For example, garlic is used heavily in most dishes. Also, noodles, common in Asia as well, get their own special treatment in Korea. The staple protein source, seafood, is cooked in styles ranging from rather plain to highly seasoned. Stir-frying, steaming, grilling, and stewing all have their place in seafood cookery, which perhaps best exemplifies Korean cuisine. Beef, the most popular meat, is cooked in various manners and is often seasoned with the flavors so beloved among Korean cooks: soy sauce, sesame oil and seeds, garlic, sugar, ginger, scallions, and chilies. Korea doesn't have the huge variety of cooking styles found in countries such as China and India, but the cuisine has developed a very nicely balanced array of dishes that uses the wonderful assortment of ingredients available.

What Makes It Korean: Special Ingredients In Korean Cuisine

THERE ARE MANY INGREDIENTS and preparations that make Korean cuisine a unique force. However, you can also find most of the same ingredients used throughout much of Asia. The most distinctive ones follow.

KOREAN SEXTET

This is simply an apt name for the six common ingredients used to season so many Korean dishes. They are garlic, ginger, soy sauce, sugar, scallions, and sesame oil and seeds. Then there's the Korean Sextet Plus, which is the Sextet plus chilies. Not all Korean dishes are seasoned this way, but these ingredients are so common that it's easier to refer to them this way than to list them individually in so many menu items.

KIMCHI

While there are many possible ingredients for this pickled dish, Chinese cabbage is by far the most common. The ingredients are salted and seasoned with chilies. Preserved in this way, *kimchi* was traditionally buried in large crocks stored for use during for winter months. *Kimchi* has provided Koreans with necessary vegetables in their diet for countless generations. Today, a meal without *kimchi* is absolutely unimaginable.

BAECHU
Essentially Chinese cabbage, similar to napa cabbage, used in cabbage *kimchi*.

BORI CHA
Roasted barley tea, which Koreans drink rather than the pekoe tea found throughout Asia.

CHAMGIREUM
Sesame oil, an absolute necessity, part of the Sextet.

CHEONGPO
A curd, similar to *tofu,* made from mung beans.

DANGMYON
Cellophane noodles made from mung bean flour or sweet potato flour.

DASHIMA
Kelp, a very popular seaweed.

DORAJI
A small root from the mountain bellflower.

DOTORI MUK
Acorn curd, more substance than taste, but full of nutrition.

DUBU
Tofu. While certainly not unique to Korea, *tofu* is absolutely essential to the Korean diet. It's interesting that a cuisine that uses so much meat also uses so much *tofu*, but this is definitely the case with Korean cuisine.

DWENJANG
A fermented soybean paste seasoned with chili pepper. An essential seasoning that adds body and depth of flavor.

EUNHAENG
Gingko nuts, from the tree that is the symbol of Korea.

GAJI
Any of a variety of eggplants.

GANJANG
Soy sauce, the main source of salt for seasoning.

GIM
Pressed laver, a seaweed, often served toasted with sesame seeds.

GOCHUJANG

A chili paste made from red chili peppers, soybean paste, and glutinous rice flour. An essential Korean seasoning.

GOSARI

Essentially, fiddleheads, although there are other types of *gosari,* which generically include other fern shoots and stems.

GUI

Grilled foods, often cooked at the table.

GYEOJA

Hot mustard, similar to the Chinese version or the Japanese *wasabi,* which quickly clears stuffed noses.

KAENNIP

The word looks like "catnip" to Americans, but it's actually sesame leaves.

MANEUL

Garlic. In no way unique to Korea, garlic is nonetheless more important to Korean cuisine than to any other in Asia. You can't eat a Korean meal without tasting large amounts of garlic.

MAREUN MYOLCHI

Dried anchovies, often deep-fried.

MAREUN OJINGEO
Dried cuttlefish, popular for snacking.

MAREUN SAEU
Dried shrimp.

MIYEOK
Browned seaweed, used in soups.

MU
Korean radish. Much milder than the American version, *mu* is nice and crisp, and is used in *kimchi*.

MYOLCHI BOKEUM
A sweet, slightly spicy condiment of dried anchovies.

NAENGMYON
Noodles made from buckwheat, essentially the same as *soba* noodles.

NAMUL
Herbs/vegetables, whether raw or cooked, that accompany every Korean meal.

SAENGGANG
Ginger root. Like garlic, one of the most common ingredients in Korean cooking.

SAEUJEOT

Fermented shrimp.

SUKGAT

Chrysanthemum leaves, used in salads and stir-fries.

SUNMU

Korean turnip, quite a mild flavor, used in *kimchi* and salads.

UEONG

Burdock root, now gaining great popularity in the United States for its healthful properties.

Appetizers and Side Dishes

A KOREAN MEAL is typically served all at once. There are special occasions in Korea that involve lengthy, multiple-course meals, but they're the exception. In Korean restaurants in the United States, some typical snack items, side dishes *(banchan),* or bar snacks might be offered as appetizers, or the meal might be broken up in other ways, but that's mostly to fit in with the American style of dining.

Why not try the authentic Korean style, and ask the server to bring all the dishes at the same time? Just order a bunch of dishes and dig in! There are certainly enough side dishes in the Korean repertoire to put together a satisfying meal. Just add rice.

BEOSEOT NAMUL

Dried mushrooms simply stir-fried.

CHABAN

Three dishes composed of dried anchovies, flying fish, and strips of beef, all marinated in the Korean Sextet.

DASHIMA TWIGIM

Fried kelp. Perhaps a bit of an acquired taste to those not used to the taste of the sea.

DUBU GUI

Tofu stuffed with seasoned beef and fried. The seasoning is basically the Korean Sextet, and the *tofu* is a great medium for absorbing the flavors.

DUBU JORIM

Tofu fried and marinated in soy sauce, chilies, garlic, and scallions.

GAJI MUCHIM

Eggplant stuffed with beef, mushrooms, nuts, and sesame seeds.

GAJI NAMUL

Marinated strips of eggplant.

GOCHU MUCHIM

A medium-hot chili pepper steamed and tossed with sesame oil and seeds. Be careful, medium hot is quite hot.

GOGUMA

Sweet potatoes cooked in their jackets.

GYERAN MARI

A mildly seasoned meat and egg loaf.

HOBAK NAMUL

Marinated strips of zucchini.

MU NAMUL

Korean radishes in a light marinade of sesame oil and seeds, salt and pepper, garlic, and sugar.

NAGCHI MUCHIM

Nicely seasoned, salted vegetables with octopus slices.

PAJEON

Pancakes. A Korean pancake can include almost any ingredient. First the batter is poured onto the griddle, then ingredients are placed on top, then it's cooked on the other side. You'll find a large variety of Korean pancakes. Be sure to order one of these tasty concoctions. A dipping sauce usually accompanies them.

SALMEUN GYERAN

Boiled eggs arranged on a bed of shredded carrots to re-semble a flower.

SOGOGI JANGJORIM

Shredded, cooked beef in soy sauce.

SUKJU NAMUL

A *namul* is any vegetable dish, raw or cooked. This one is fresh bean sprouts seasoned with sesame oil and seeds, gar-lic, and scallions.

SUNDAE

Seasoned rice with beef or pork blood stuffed in a pig's in-testine and cooked.

TWIGIM

Fritters. Along with *pajeon* (pancakes), *twigim* are extremely popular Korean snack items. Essentially the same as American-style fritters, the ingredients can be almost any-thing. A delicious accompaniment to a meal.

YUKHOE

Marinated strips of raw beef, very tasty. Sort of a Korean *carpaccio*.

Seafood Dishes

SEAFOOD IS VERY important to Korean cuisine. Surrounded by water, Korea has developed innumerable delicious fish concoctions. Fish is the primary source of protein for Koreans, and Korean preparations do it great justice.

AL JIGAE OR AL TANG

A soup, or hot pot, of fish roe and vegetables, simply cooked in water and only lightly seasoned. The idea is to accentuate the flavor of the roe.

BUGEO GUI

Spicy and sweet pollock, made from dried fish that is rehydrated. The Korean Sextet is the marinade, with a greater emphasis on the sweetness. The fish is grilled and the texture is chewy. It's more of an acquired taste than some dishes, but worth a try.

DAEGU TANG

Cod cooked in water with vegetables and *tofu,* seasoned with ginger and garlic. A sort of soup/stew, frequently known as a hot pot, this is a family-style dish that allows the individual ingredients to shine.

DAEHAP YANG NYEOM GUI

Clams chopped up and mixed with the Korean Sextet Plus, returned to the half shells, and baked.

DOMI JIM

Red snapper stuffed with ground, seasoned beef, then steamed, and garnished with julienne vegetables and strips of omelette.

GYE JANG

Marinated raw crab, seasoned with the Korean Sextet, and served as a side dish.

GYE JIM

Crab mixed with *tofu* and beef, seasoned, and steamed in the crab shells. A very nice treatment for the crab, and normal garnishes on the platter are cucumbers and strips of omelette.

GYE TANG

Crabs stewed with the Korean Sextet Plus, along with onions and squash. The dish is served with rice, as usual. Crab blends especially well with Korean spices, and this great dish is rich and spicy at the same time.

HAESANMUL JEONGOL

A grand celebration dish composed of 21 ingredients laid out in a careful and colorful way. Beef, seafood, and vegetables are beautifully arranged and then simmered in broth. Diners help themselves, much in the same way as with *sukiyaki*.

JEONBOK JUK
Thick soup made from abalone and rice.

MAEUN OJINGEO BOKEUM
Squid stir-fried with assorted vegetables, highly seasoned with chilies, and served with *soba* noodles.

NAGCHI HOE
Raw octopus with a dip made of the Korean Sextet, shrimp paste, and vinegar.

OJINGEO BOKEUM
Squid and mushrooms stir-fried with snow peas and seasoned lightly.

OJINGEO HOE
Raw squid with dip made from the Korean Sextet and vinegar.

OJINGEO PO MUCHIM
Dried raw squid, shredded and seasoned.

OJINGEO SUNDAE
Squid sausage, quite spicy.

SAENGSEON BULGOGI

Barbecued fish, rubbed with a mixture of soy sauce, chili paste, sugar, pepper, sesame seeds, sesame oil, garlic, and ginger, then grilled. This dish is a great example of Korean barbecue using fish rather than beef or chicken.

SAENGSEON GUI

Grilled fish, usually an oily type, with soy sauce, chilies, and sesame seeds. The accompaniments provide the necessary complementary flavors for the more strongly flavored fish.

SAENGSEON HOE

Sliced raw fish served with dipping sauces, generally a fiery-hot pepper sauce and a mustard-vinegar sauce.

SAENGSEON JEON

Fried fish, a very simple dish in which fish fillets are dipped in egg batter and fried, served with a light dipping sauce.

SAENGSEON JIM

A whole fish that has been steamed, then fried, and seasoned with sesame seeds, ginger, garlic, and soy sauce. Served with lots of side garnishes, this is an impressive-looking dish, with a great texture.

SAENGSEON JUK

Rice with fish broth, made from freshwater fish. The soup is seasoned with the Korean Sextet.

SAENGSEON SANJEOK

A combination of fish and beef, skewered, marinated, and grilled. Korean cuisine frequently combines meat and seafood, and this Korean answer to the *shish kebab* is a tasty meal indeed.

SAENGSEON YANG NYEOM GUI

A whole fish rubbed with salt, oil, soy sauce, chili, garlic, sesame seeds, and scallions, then grilled. The crust is spicy and aromatic.

SAEU GUI

Shrimp stuffed with beef and *tofu,* seasoned, and broiled.

SAEU JIM

Garnished shrimp that are steamed. The garnishes are typically strips of vegetables that add a nice color, usually carrots, tree ears, and cucumbers, as well as omelette strips. This dish is not seasoned with anything, as the naturally sweet taste of the shrimp is meant to shine through.

Meat and Poultry Dishes

BEEF IS EXTREMELY popular in Korean cuisine. Traditionally very expensive in Korea, and still much more expensive than seafood, beef is highly prized. Pork and chicken have been mainstays in the northern parts, beef in the South. As with seafood, meat is most usually seasoned with the Korean Sextet, and often with chilies. Cider vinegar is also a common ingredient, which adds a nice acidic balance to the saltiness of the soy sauce and the sweetness of the sugar. Also, the vinegar helps to balance and round out the heat from the chilies.

BANGJA GUI
Slices of beef seasoned and grilled, eaten wrapped in a lettuce leaf.

BULGOGI
The beef is raw, and the dressing is hot and sour, basically the traditional Korean Sextet. Practically the national dish of Korea, *bulgogi* is beef marinated in soy sauce, garlic, pepper, scallions, sugar, and sesame oil (no ginger!), then grilled. A very basic dish, it nicely illustrates the Korean philosophy of seasoning meats and other foods. *Bulgogi* is normally served with rice and other side dishes.

BULGOGI NEUTARI BEOSEOT BOKEUM
Skewered beef with some agaric *neutari,* a Korean fungus with tentacles.

DAK BULGOGI
Grilled chicken seasoned with soy sauce, scallions, ginger, garlic, sugar, and pepper.

DAK GOCHUJANG BOKEUM
Chicken marinated and simmered in a hot sauce. The extra chili pepper is a great foil to the sesame-garlic-soy sauce combination.

DAK JIM

Chicken stew with carrots and potatoes.

DON KAS

Pork cutlet breaded and pan-fried. Mildly seasoned with garlic, ginger, salt, and pepper, this is a simple treatment that complements pork well.

DWEJI GALBI GUI

Pork spareribs barbecued with the usual Korean spices. This is a particularly satisfying taste combination.

GALBI GUI

An expensive alternative to *bulgogi,* it uses rib steaks.

GALBI JIM

Braised beef short ribs with chestnuts and mushrooms. The chestnuts go especially well with the Korean seasonings, adding a sweet, nutty flavor. This is really one of the great tasting dishes in Korean cuisine's repertoire.

GANJEON

Veal liver cutlet, dipped in egg batter and panfried. Very simply seasoned with salt and pepper, this is a wonderful dish for relieving the overwhelmed palate.

JEYUK BOKEUM

Strips of pork sautéed with potatoes and all the Korean spices. The potatoes add a lovely touch, absorbing the flavors while maintaining their own character.

JEYUK GUI

Three-layer pork, marinated and grilled. This cut of pork is used throughout Asia. Three-layer pork is composed of the outer layer of skin, a thick layer of fat, and a layer of lean meat.

SOGOGI KAS

Breaded and panfried beef cutlets.

SOGOGI PYOGO BEOSEOT BOKEUM

Beef stir-fried with dried mushrooms, which are similar in taste to dried *shiitakes*.

SOKORI JIM

A simple oxtail stew, not excessively seasoned.

YEONG GYE BAEK SUK

Game hens stuffed with rice and cooked in a highly aromatic broth with garlic, ginseng, ginger, jujubes, chestnuts, and scallions. The broth is clear and strong.

YUK HOE

Sort of a Korean version of *carpaccio*, although the meat isn't cut as thinly.

YUK SANJEOK

A Korean version of *shish kebab*. The skewered beef is marinated in the Korean Sextet with a lot of black pepper, and sautéed.

Rice and Noodle Dishes

RICE IS THE TRADITIONAL staple food of Korea and is eaten in large quantities. Usually a medium-grain sticky rice, it can be eaten with chopsticks or a soup spoon. Eaten as part of a meal, the simply prepared, steamed rice is a wonderful counterbalance to highly seasoned dishes. In addition, several interesting rice dishes are made that can be eaten on their own or as part of a larger meal.

Noodles, at one time considered food only fit for people unable to afford rice, are now an integral part of Korean cuisine. Wheat, rice, and buckwheat are common ingredients in Korean noodles. Be sure to try the delicious noodle dishes that have become part of Korean cooking.

BAB

Steamed rice, the most common way to eat rice in Korea.

BAM BAB

Rice and chestnuts cooked together. The natural sweetness of the two ingredients makes a dish that is a great complement to other types of dishes.

BIBIMBAB

Rice and various vegetable and meat garnishes, generally served in a clay pot. The garnishes are piled up on the rice and can be stirred into it before eating.

GUKSU

A favorite noodle dish among Koreans, and a real comfort food. Basically, noodles and beef broth with sliced cooked steak or another meat, as well as cucumbers, spinach, omelette strips, and scallions. Despite its Korean character, this dish is similar to Vietnamese noodle dishes.

JAB CHAE

A very popular noodle dish, which can be prepared with any number of vegetables and meats. Korean vermicelli or *danmyon,* made from sweet potatoes and starch, is the standard noodle for this dish. Other types may be substituted. The ingredients are all stir-fried and mixed with the cooked noodles, similar to Chinese *lo mein.*

NAENGMYON

A sort of pasta salad made with buckwheat noodles, much like Japanese *soba* noodles. Various garnishes are prepared and served with the noodles, either on top, on the side, or mixed in already. The seasoning is basically the Korean Sextet. There are two kinds of *naengmyon: bibim naengmyon* and *mul naengmyon.*

OGOK BAB

Rice with barley, millet, sorghum, and soybeans, all cooked together. Not only is this dish a pleasant diversion from spicier foods, it's good for you, too!

PAT BAB

The Korean version of red beans and rice, nothing like the American dish from the South. These red beans are the small Asian variety, and the only seasoning is a little salt. A pleasant, healthy dish.

Glossary

MEATS

Beef—*Sogogi*

Anshim	Fillet
Chateaubriand	Chateaubriand
Delmonico	Delmonico
Deungshim	Sirloin
Filet mignon	Filet mignon
Galbi	Rib
Gan	Liver
Heobeokji sal	Round
Moksal	Chuck
Porterhouse	Porterhouse
Steak	Steak
Teuk galbi	Prime rib
Yeomtong	Heart
Yeopgurisal steak	Flank steak

Lamb—*Yanggogi*

Chop	Chop
Deungshim	Saddle
Eokaesal	Shoulder
Galbi chop	Rib chop
Heorisal	Loin
Herisal chop	Loin chop
Mokdeolmi gogi	Rack

| *Satae* | Shank |
| *Yanggogi* | Mutton |

Pork—*Tejigogi*

Barbeque galbi	Barbecued spareribs
Chop	Chop
Galbi	Spareribs
Ham	Ham
Heorisal	Loin
Hunje ham	Smoked ham
Ipsul	Lips

Chicken—*Takgogi*

Amtak	Hen
Dakdari	Drumstick
Dari	Leg
Gan	Liver
Gaseum sal	Breast
Heobeokji sal	Thigh
Kas	Cutlet
Naejang	Giblets
Nalgae	Wings
Pyeoeomneun gaseum sal	Boneless breast
Sutak	Capon
Wijang	Gizzard

Turkey—*Tokigogi*

Dajin chilmyonjo gogi	Ground turkey
Gaseum sal	Breast
Kas	Cutlet

Veal—*Songaji gogi*

Chejang sal	Sweetbreads
Chop	Chop
Cutlet	Cutlet
Dari	Leg
Eokaesal	Shoulder
Gan	Liver
Gaseum	Breast
Heorisal	Loin
Kongpat	Kidneys
Satae	Shank

Goat—*Yomsogogi*

Chop	Chop
Deungsal	Saddle

Poultry—*Ka gyeom egogi*

Bidulgi	Squab (pigeon)
Geowi	Goose
Jago	Partridge
Kwong	Pheasant
Mechuri	Quail

Ori	Duck
Tajo	Ostrich

Game—*Ki ryu ko it neon chimseong te*

Dweji	Boar
Saseum	Venison
Sunlok	Reindeer
Toki	Rabbit

SEAFOOD

Fin fish—*Seng seon*

Agui	Monkfish
Chamchi	Tuna
Cheolgapsangeo	Sturgeon
Cheongeo	Herring
Cheongeomuri	Shad
Daegu	Cod
Daegumuri	Pollock
Daegusaeki	Scrod
Dalgogi	John Dory
Domi	Red snapper
Gajami	Flounder
Gereuchi	Bluefish
Godeungeo	Mackerel
Grouper	Grouper
Haddock	Haddock
Hwangsaechi	Swordfish
Hyeoneopchi	Sole

Jangeo	Eel
Jeongaengi	Pompano
Jeongeori	Sardine
Mahi-mahi	Mahimahi
Mareun myolchi	Dried anchovies
Mareun saeu	Dried shrimp
Meg	Catfish
Neopchi	Halibut, turbot
Nongeo	Bass, striped bass
Orange roughy	Orange roughy
Sangeo	Shark
Songeo	Whitefish
Sungeo	Trout
Yeoneo	Salmon

Shellfish—*Kap kan yu*

Badatgajae	Lobster
Chamsaeu	Prawn
Daeha; wangsaeu	Crayfish
Daehap	Clam
Garibi	Scallop
Ge	Crab
Gul	Oyster
Honghap	Mussel
Jeonbok	Abalone
Jogabi	Conch
Mareun ojingeo	Dried cuttlefish

Muneo	Octopus
Ojingeo	Cuttlefish, squid
Saejogae	Cockle
Saeu	Shrimp

DAIRY PRODUCTS

Butter	Butter
Butter gireum	Ghee
Buttermilk	Buttermilk
Cream	Cream
Crème fraîche	Crème fraîche
Eunggo cream	Clotted cream
Geopum cream	Whipped cream
Gyeran	Egg
Half-and-half	Half-and-half
Ice cream	Ice cream
Jeojibang uyu	Nonfat milk
Margarine	Margarine
Saeng uyu	Whole milk
Shin cream	Sour cream
Uyu	Milk
Yogurt	Yogurt

VEGETABLES

Baechu	Chinese cabbage
Banjeom kong	Pinto bean
Beoseot	Mushroom
Bok choy	Bok choy

Buchu	Leek
Celery	Celery
Celery puri	Celery root (celeriac)
Chamma	Yam
Cornell oi	Cornell cucumber
Dan huchu	Sweet pepper
Danggeun	Carrot
Dashima	Kelp
Doraji	Mountain bellflower root
Gaji	Eggplant
Galanga puri	Galanga root (galangal)
Gamja	Potato
Geomeun kong	Black bean
Goguma	Sweet potato
Gosari	Fiddleheads or fern shoots and stems
Gugyeongyang-baechu	Kohlrabi
Gyeoja	Mustard
Gyeowul hobak	Winter squash
Hayan kong	White bean
Heuin kong	Kidney bean
Hobak	Pumpkin
Hoehyang	Fennel
Huchu	Pepper
Jageun oksusu	Baby corn
Jageun yachae	Baby vegetable

Kaennip	Sesame leaves
Kaffir lime	Kaffir lime
Kaffir lime ip	Kaffir lime leaf
Kong	Bean
Kong sak	Bean sprouts
Kotyangbaechu	Cauliflower
Kwari	Tomatillo
Maeun huchu	Hot pepper
Maneul	Garlic
Mu	Radish, Korean radish
Napjakhan kong	Snow pea
Pa	Scallion
Paengi beoseot	Straw mushroom
Parsnip	Parsnip
Saenggang	Ginger root
Satangmu	Beet
Seoyang hobak	Summer squash, zucchini
Shallot	Shallot
Shigeumchi	Spinach
Someonggeongkwi	Artichoke
Sukgat	Chrysanthemum leaves
Sunmu	Rutabaga, turnip, Korean turnip
Suyeong	Sorrel
Tomato	Tomato
Ueong	Burdock root
Wandukong	Pea
Yangbaechu	Cabbage, kale

Yangpa	Onion
Yasaeng beoseot	Wild mushroom

FRUITS

Aengdu	Cherry
Bae	Pear
Banana	Banana
Blackberry	Blackberry
Blueberry	Blueberry
Boksunga	Peach
Casaba	Casaba
Crenshaw	Crenshaw
Daechuyaja	Date
Daehwang	Rhubarb
Gam	Persimmon
Gamromeron	Honeydew
Geumgyul	Kumquat
Jadu	Plum
Janggwa	Berry
Kiwi fruit	Kiwifruit
Lemon	Lemon
Lime	Lime
Mango	Mango
Melon	Melon
Meron	Cantaloupe
Mogwa	Quince
Muhwagwa	Fig

Neonchulwolgyul	Cranberry
Orange	Orange
Papaya	Papaya
Pineapple	Pineapple
Podo	Grape
Sagwa	Apple
Salgu	Apricot
Santalgi	Raspberry
Seongnu	Pomegranate
Seoyang bae	Prickly pear
Seungdoboksunga	Nectarine
Star fruit	Star fruit
Subak	Watermelon
Talgi	Strawberry
Tanghereu orange	Tangerine

GRAINS

Basmati sal	Basmati rice
Bori	Barley
Garu	Grits
Guiri	Oats
Gulgegan oksusu	Hominy
Heon mi sal	Brown rice
Heuin sal	White rice
Jasmine sal	Jasmine rice
Masa	Harina
Memil	Buckwheat

Mil	Wheat
Oksusugaru	Cornmeal
Sal	Rice
Wild sal	Wild rice

HERBS AND SPICES

Baekrihyang	Thyme
Bakha	Mint
Bunhong huchu yolmae	Pink peppercorn
Chamkae si	Sesame seed
Cheungcheung	Savory
Dan gochu	Paprika
Gaesacheolsuk	Tarragon
Gobhyangnamu	Juniper
Gochu	Cayenne, chilies
Gochutgaru	Chili powder
Golpa	Chives
Gosuip	Cilantro
Gyeoja si	Mustard seed
Gyepi	Cinnamon
Hoehyang	Fennel
Hoehyangpul	Caraway
Horopa	Fenugreek
Huchu yolmae	Peppercorn
Inond	Dill
Jageun saenggang	Lesser ginger

Jeonghyang	Clove
Kare	Curry
Mayorana	Marjoram
Myeongaju	Epazote
Nareukpul	Basil
Saenggang	Ginger
Shimhwang	Turmeric
Star anise	Star anise
Wolgyesu	Bay leaf, laurel
Yangguibi si	Poppy seed
Yukdugu	Nutmeg

NUTS

Bam	Chestnut
Eunhaeng	Gingko nuts
Hodu	Walnut
Macadamia	Macadamia nut
Pecan	Pecan
Pistachio	Pistachio
Sonamu gyeongwa	Pine nut
Tangkong	Peanut

MISCELLANEOUS INGREDIENTS & TERMS

Balsamic shikcho	Balsamic vinegar
Bori cha	Roasted barley tea
Chamgireum	Sesame oil
Cheongpo	Mung bean curd
Chorok olive	Green olives

Dangmyon	Cellophane noodles made from mung bean flour or sweet potato flour
Dotori muk	Acorn curd
Dubu	*Tofu*
Dwenjang	Fermented soybean paste with chilies
Ganjang	Soy sauce
Geomeun olive	Black olives (ripe)
Gim	Pressed *laver* (a seaweed)
Gireum	Oil
Gochujang	Chili paste with soybean paste and glutinous rice flour
Gui	Grilled foods, often cooked at the table
Gyeoja	Mustard
Kalamata olive	Kalamata olives
Ketchup	Ketchup
Kimchi	Pickled vegetables, most notably cabbage, with pronounced spiciness from chilies
Miyeok	Browned seaweed
Naengmyon	Buckwheat noodles, similar to Japanese *soba*
Namul	Vegetables, either raw or cooked, that accompany every Korean meal
Nicoise olive	Niçoise olives
Olive yu	Olive oil

Saengseon sauce	Fish sauce
Sal guksu	Rice noodles
Shikcho	Vinegar
Sogeum	Salt
Somyon	Thin wheat noodles
Wine shikcho	Wine vinegar
Wusteo sauce	Worcestershire sauce
Yanggochunaengi	Horseradish

SPECIAL DIETS

Allergic	Allergic
Allergy	Allergy
Chaesikjuija	Vegetarian
Cheoljeohan chaesikjuija	Vegan
Go seomyu	High-fiber
Gwasikjuija	Fruitarian
Jayeonshik	Macrobiotic
Jeo calorie	Low-calorie
Jeo dangbun	Low-sodium
Jeo jibang	Low-fat
Lactose intolerant	Lactose intolerant
Mil allergy	Wheat allergy
Mu bujil	Wheat/gluten free
Mu jibang	Nonfat
Mu seoltang	Sugar free
Mu yuga	Dairy free

Appendix: Pronunciation Keys

(Vowels and consonants not listed in each
key have similar sounds to the English.)

JAPANESE PRONUNCIATION KEY

VOWELS

a	as in f**a**ther
ai	as in g**uy**
e	as in b**e**t
ei	as in s**ay**
i	as in gr**ee**n
o	as in t**o**te
oi	as in Chl**oe**
u	as in fl**u**te
ui	as in u in p**u**t followed quickly by ee in s**ee**

CONSONANTS

f	between an English f in **f**inish and h in **h**appy
g	as in si**ng**
j	as in **J**apan
r	between an English l in **l**ight and r in **r**owboat
ts	as in ho**t** + **s**un

LAO PRONUNCIATION KEY

VOWELS

ai	as in Thai
ae	as in ham
ao	as in allow
ea	as in bean
eui	as in Louie
eu	as in push
ii	as in keen
ia	as in yarn
ua	as in water
uai	as in choir
uu	as in soon

CONSONANTS

k	as in look
kh	as in carry
ng	as in sing
nh	as in pan
p	as in tap
ph	as in party
t	as in stick
th	as in take
x	as in cats

CAMBODIAN PRONUNCIATION KEY

VOWELS

a	as in father
ai	as in Thai
aeu	as in **ah + you** (with a closed "you")
ao	as in allow
au	as in paw
ay	as in play
e	as in pet
ea	as in seance
eau	as in **eau** de cologne
ee	as in keen
ei	as in play
eu	as in **you,** but more closed, as in the French *yeux*
i	as in hit
ia	as in yarn
o	as in possible
oa	as in boa
oeu	as in push, but more rounded
oi	as in boy
oo	as in soon
u	as in sun
ua	as in water
uai	as in choir

CONSONANTS

j	as in **j**ester
k	as in **c**arry
kh	as in knoc**k** + **h**im
ng	as in si**ng**
nj	as in me**n**u
p	as in ta**p**
ph	as in hi**p** + **h**ip
t	as in s**t**ick
th	as in **t**ab
tj	as in hi**t** + **y**ou
tz	as in ca**ts**

MALAY & INDONESIAN PRONUNCIATION KEY

VOWELS

a	as in f**a**ther
ai	as in turk**ey** (when it appears at the end of a word)
ao	as in L**ao**s, or sp**a**+**o**pening
au	as in c**ow**
e	as in t**ou**ch
eo	as in m**ayo**
i	either as in p**i**tch *(mentimun),* or as in s**ee** *(ikan)*
ia	as in **i**s + **o**n, minus the "s" and "n"
ing	as in s**ing**

PRONUNCIATION KEYS

o	as in n**o**
u	as in s**oo**n
ua	as in **wa**ter

CONSONANTS

c	as in **ch**ess
j	as in **j**ust
ngk	as in thi**nk**

THAI PRONUNCIATION KEY

VOWELS

a	as in f**a**ther
ae	as in c**a**t
ai	as in Th**ai**
ao	as in h**ow**
ay	as in hoor**ay**
e	as in g**e**t
eaw	as in **yaw**n
eiw	as in g**ray** + **wh**ale
ee	as in g**a**te
i	as in h**i**t
ii	as in f**ee**t
o	as in l**o**g**o**
oi	as in b**oy**
oo	as in s**o**
u	as in c**ou**ld

ua	as in foie gras
uea	as in way + up
uu	as in too

CONSONANTS

c	as in Spanish *cincilla*
ch	as in church
j	as in jester
k	as in skin
kh	as in kin
ng	as in sing
p	as in spin
ph	as in pin
t	as in still
th	as in till

VIETNAMESE PRONUNCIATION KEY

VOWELS

a	as in father
ai	as in Thai
ao	as in how
au	as in auburn
ay	as in day
e	as in fair
i	as in see
ia	as in amnesia

ie	as in **ye**s
ieu	as in **ewe**
o	as in fl**oor**
oa	as in French *m**oi***
oai	as in **why**
oay	as in Urug**uay**
oe	as in **whe**ther
oi	as in v**oi**ce
u	as in fl**u**te
ua	as in Ec**ua**dor
ui	as in Lo**ui**e
uo	as in q**uo**te
uy	as **u** in French or **ü** in German
uya	as French cult**ure**
uyen	as in wh**en**
uyu	as in n**ew**
y	as in s**ee**
ye	as in **ye**n
yeu	as in **yeo**man

CONSONANTS

d	as in **z**ero
gh	as in **g**o
gi	as in **cz**ar, with a **y**es sound following the consonant
kh	as in Ba**ch**
nh	as in Russian *n**y**et*

ng, ngh	as in **Ng**uyen
ph	as in **f**un
x	as in **s**een

KOREAN PRONUNCIATION KEY

VOWELS

a	as in f**a**ther
ae	as in b**a**t
e	as in b**ai**t
eo	as in lem**o**n
eu	as in ros**e**s
i	as in b**ea**t
o	as in d**oo**r
u	as in f**oo**d
wa	as in **wa**nt
wi	as in **wee**p
wo	as in **wa**ll
ya	as in **ya**rd
yeo	as in **yea**rn
yo	as in **ya**cht
yu	as in **you**

CONSONANTS

b	as in **b**ed
ch	as in **ch**urch
d	as in **d**og

PRONUNCIATION KEYS

g	as in **g**ame
h	as in **h**ouse
j	as in **z**oo
k	as in **k**ing
kk	as in s**c**ream
l	as in **l**ong
m	as in **m**other
n	as in **n**ice
ng	as in so**ng**
p	as in **p**ie
pp	as in s**p**ring
r	as in **r**ock
s	as in **s**in
sh	as in **sh**ield
t	as in **t**ime
tt	as in s**t**eak

Tipping Chart

TOTAL	15%	20%	TOTAL	15%	20%
$5	0.75	$1.00	$24	$3.60	$4.80
$6	$0.90	$1.20	$25	$3.75	$5.00
$7	$1.05	$1.40	$26	$3.90	$5.20
$8	$1.20	$1.60	$27	$4.05	$5.40
$9	$1.35	$1.80	$28	$4.20	$5.60
$10	$1.50	$2.00	$29	$4.35	$5.80
$11	$1.65	$2.20	$30	$4.50	$6.00
$12	$1.80	$2.40	$31	$4.65	$6.20
$13	$1.95	$2.60	$32	$4.80	$6.40
$14	$2.10	$2.80	$33	$4.95	$6.60
$15	$2.25	$3.00	$34	$5.10	$6.80
$16	$2.40	$3.20	$35	$5.25	$7.00
$17	$2.55	$3.40	$36	$5.40	$7.20
$18	$2.70	$3.60	$37	$5.55	$7.40
$19	$2.85	$3.80	$38	$5.70	$7.60
$20	$3.00	$4.00	$39	$5.85	$7.80
$21	$3.15	$4.20	$40	$6.00	$8.00
$22	$3.30	$4.40	$41	$6.15	$8.20
$23	$3.45	$4.60	$42	$6.30	$8.40

TIPPING CHART

TOTAL	15%	20%	TOTAL	15%	20%
$43	$6.45	$8.60	$64	$9.60	$12.80
$44	$6.60	$8.80	$65	$9.75	$13.00
$45	$6.75	$9.00	$66	$9.90	$13.20
$46	$6.90	$9.20	$67	$10.05	$13.40
$47	$7.05	$9.40	$68	$10.20	$13.60
$48	$7.20	$9.60	$69	$10.35	$13.80
$49	$7.35	$9.80	$70	$10.50	$14.00
$50	$7.50	$10.00	$71	$10.65	$14.20
$51	$7.65	$10.20	$72	$10.80	$14.40
$52	$7.80	$10.40	$73	$10.95	$14.60
$53	$7.95	$10.60	$74	$11.10	$14.80
$54	$8.10	$10.80	$75	$11.25	$15.00
$55	$8.25	$11.00	$76	$11.40	$15.20
$56	$8.40	$11.20	$77	$11.55	$15.40
$57	$8.55	$11.40	$78	$11.70	$15.60
$58	$8.70	$11.60	$79	$11.85	$15.80
$59	$8.85	$11.80	$80	$12.00	$16.00
$60	$9.00	$12.00	$81	$12.15	$16.20
$61	$9.15	$12.20	$82	$12.30	$16.40
$62	$9.30	$12.40	$83	$12.45	$16.60
$63	$9.45	$12.60	$84	$12.60	$16.80

TOTAL	15%	20%	TOTAL	15%	20%
$85	$12.75	$17.00	$107	$16.05	$21.40
$86	$12.90	$17.20	$108	$16.20	$21.60
$87	$13.05	$17.40	$109	$15.35	$21.80
$89	$13.35	$17.80	$110	$16.50	$22.00
$90	$13.50	$18.00	$111	$16.65	$22.20
$91	$13.65	$18.20	$112	$16.80	$22.40
$92	$13.80	$18.40	$113	$16.95	$22.60
$93	$13.95	$18.60	$114	$17.10	$22.80
$94	$14.10	$18.80	$115	$17.25	$23.00
$95	$14.25	$19.00	$116	$17.40	$23.20
$96	$14.40	$19.20	$117	$17.55	$23.40
$97	$14.55	$19.40	$118	$17.70	$23.60
$98	$14.70	$19.60	$119	$17.85	$23.80
$99	$14.85	$15.00	$120	$18.00	$24.00
$100	$15.00	$20.00	$121	$18.15	$24.20
$101	$15.15	$20.20	$122	$18.30	$24.40
$102	$15.30	$20.40	$123	$18.45	$24.60
$103	$15.45	$20.60	$124	$18.60	$24.80
$104	$15.60	$20.80	$125	$18.75	$25.00
$105	$15.75	$21.00	$126	$18.90	$25.20
$106	$15.90	$21.20	$127	$19.05	$25.40

TIPPING CHART

TOTAL	15%	20%	TOTAL	15%	20%
$128	$19.20	$25.60	$134	$20.10	$26.80
$129	$19.35	$25.80	$135	$20.25	$27.00
$130	$19.50	$26.00	$136	$20.40	$27.20
$131	$19.65	$26.20	$137	$20.55	$27.40
$132	$19.80	$26.40	$138	$20.70	$27.60
$133	$19.95	$26.60			

About the Author

David D'Aprix began his cooking career at the age of seven, when he prepared his first batch of oatmeal. Fifteen years later, after completing a Bachelor of Arts degree in liberal arts, D'Aprix remembered the thrill of making that porridge. He enrolled in the Culinary Institute of America and graduated in 1977. In addition to extensive experience in the hotel and restaurant industries, D'Aprix has been on the faculty in the School of Hotel Administration at Cornell University, where he currently lectures, and he has given seminars in many countries throughout the world. He lives in Ithaca, New York, with his wife and two children.